Fingerstyle Blues G

Master Acoustic Blues Guitar Fingerpicking

Published by www.fundamental-changes.com

ISBN: 978-1-910403-33-4

www.fundamental-changes.com

Cover Image Copyright: Bizoo_n

Other Books from Fundamental Changes

Contents

Introduction

The blues is at the root of all modern rock, pop and jazz music and became popularised on the guitar around the turn of the 20th century. Some notable artists who popularised early blues guitar were "Mississippi" Fred McDowell, Lead Belly, Blind Lemon Jefferson, Blind Blake and Charlie Patton. These players were among the first to record and preserve the musical tradition of early acoustic blues.

While the music of these players varied, there were certain things that linked their styles and approaches. The first and most obvious factor was that they intricately wove chords, bass lines, and single line soloing into one cohesive piece of music. It can often sound like two, or even three guitars are playing at the same time. On top of this complex instrumental texture, the vocals of these blues musicians made powerful use of microtones and 'blue' notes to squeeze every ounce of emotion out of the melodies and lyrical content that was deeply rooted in everyday life, loss, slavery and emancipation. By the 1920s when recordings of these artists began to find popularity it was still debatable whether freedom was an actual reality after the emancipation in 1863.

As modern solo guitarists, learning to play acoustic blues guitar in this early style has some great benefits. Not least of these benefits is the ability to accompany ourselves when there is no band or backing track to help us. As a young electric guitarist and terrible singer, I was always stuck for something to play when people asked me to demonstrate my so-called 'talents'. Strumming the chords to Oasis songs will only get you so far if you can't sing the melody, and I always needed a backing track and PA to demonstrate the rock guitar soloing on which I worked incessantly.

Over time, I gravitated towards acoustic blues and jazz chord melody because it meant I could simply pick up a guitar and play chords, bass and lead all at the same time. No singing required! It was like being my own band and backing track.

Emulating the early acoustic blues style can be challenging because modern guitarists can be over-reliant on the pick (plectrum) when playing the guitar. The heart of the acoustic blues is independence between the thumb (or pick) and the fingers, and the development of this technique is the core of this book.

Fingerstyle Blues Guitar is split into two halves that guide you through the rudimental techniques, concepts and exercises and will turn you into an excellent acoustic blues guitarist.

Part One focuses on building your acoustic blues soloing and combining it with a steady bass line. It may seem counterintuitive to begin here rather than with chord progressions, but the technique required to mix bass lines and melodies often takes a lot of concentration and practice. The work done in this section will help you to quickly build the more complicated chord techniques in part two.

In Part One, we start from absolute basics and master the rudiments of acoustic blues: coordination, rhythm, scales, technique, articulation, and of course, maintain a constant bass line. Each aspect of playing is introduced logically and musically. The first few exercises may seem basic and boring, but these foundations quickly build into something solid and musical. Even if it seems a little obvious, every exercise is carefully designed to develop control and independence in your playing.

After working through Part One, you will be competent and musical when combining bass lines and blues guitar licks.

Part Two of this book delves deep into the other side of fingerstyle blues guitar; chords. In this section, you will learn how to play essential progressions, turnarounds, chord voicings and picking patterns while all the time combining these techniques with alternating and walking bass lines.

By combining the ideas in both parts of Fingerstyle Blues Guitar, you will quickly become adept at improvising, playing, and writing authentic-sounding acoustic blues.

Learning to play this style of music was once a big challenge for me, as the technique and approach was completely different from anything I'd played before. Even having an early start in classical guitar didn't help because the movement of the thumb in fingerstyle blues was very different from the classical approach. The solution I found was to proceed *extremely* slowly and train my fingers to play what I wanted, and *only* what I wanted. It's easy to lose focus and allow the fingers to start dictating the music. At first you must work very slowly and be incredibly deliberate about every single note. This is the only real way to develop the necessary independence in your fingers.

That said, if you persevere you will quickly find acoustic blues an incredibly fun, rewarding and impressive way to be expressive on the guitar. This style of playing will really set you apart from other guitarists and help you develop a unique approach to music that will give you a lifetime of pleasure.

Enjoy the journey and have fun.

Joseph

Get the Audio

The audio files for this book are available to download for free from **www.fundamental-changes.com** and the link is in the top right corner. Simply select this book title from the drop-down menu and follow the instructions to get the audio.

We recommend that you download the files directly to your computer, not to your tablet, and extract them there before adding them to your media library. You can then put them on your tablet, iPod or burn them to CD. On the download page there is a help PDF and we also provide technical support via the contact form.

Part One: Finger Independence and Soloing

In this section, you will build the finger independence and control that is essential for playing fingerstyle blues guitar, but instead of learning lots of boring technical exercises, these skills are taught through fun and usable musical vocabulary.

This section covers:

- *Rudimentary exercises*
- *Finger independence skills,*
- *Essential scales*
- *Pedal Bass Notes*
- *Expressive techniques*
- *Bends*
- *Slides*
- *Double-stops*
- *Hammer-ons*
- *Pull-offs*
- *Vibrato*
- *1/8th note and 1/16th note syncopation*
- *Straight and triplet feels*
- *Licks over different chords*

By mastering these skills in the first section, it will make the challenges of the rhythm playing in the second section much easier. Of course, you can dive straight into the second section whenever you want, but I recommend that you first spend some time here developing your skills and control while learning some cool licks and real music.

Chapter One: Rudiments and Finger Independence

The most important technique to master in acoustic fingerstyle blues guitar is the independence between the thumb and fingers of the picking hand, and the bass and melody parts in the fretting hand.

The exercises in this chapter will gradually help you to develop this intricate type of control. It's not the most musical playing you will ever do, but I promise that it will help your skills develop much more quickly throughout the rest of the book.

In the picking hand, you need to make a decision whether are going to use your thumb to take care of the bass notes or whether you are going to *hybrid* pick. Hybrid picking is a technique where you hold the pick (plectrum) normally between the thumb and index finger and use the spare fingers of that hand to pick the notes on the higher strings.

Neither technique is better; however using your thumb is probably more authentic of the style. Hybrid picking does create a much more distinct tone in the bass though, so have a play and decide what you like the sound of once you have mastered a few exercises and licks.

The first example is very simple. The idea is to use the thumb of the picking hand to play the note E as 1/4 notes and keep time for a few bars. Try resting the heel of the picking hand gently on the bass E string to create a palm-muted effect. We will gradually layer more techniques against this bass line. Use your thumb to play the following figure.

The absolute number one rule throughout every example in this book is to *tap your foot on the beat.* This way, your foot will always sync up with a thumb pick on the bass string. The physical movement of tapping your foot will keep your whole body in time and allow you to feel where each bass pick should be, freeing up your mind to think about the melody. This skill may take time, but it should be your highest priority.

Example 1a:

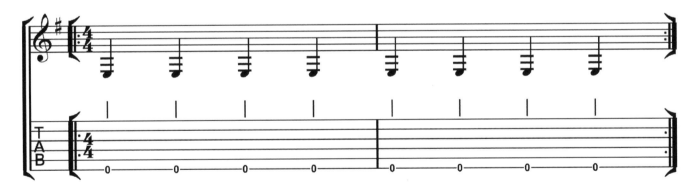

If you're new to this style you may find even this challenging at first. Stick with it until you feel relaxed and comfortable. Focus on your breathing and look around as you listen to the sound of the note. Don't forget to tap your foot.

Next, we will add a repeating E melody note that is also played in 1/4 notes. I use my ring finger for this note but you should experiment by using different fingers.

Example 1b:

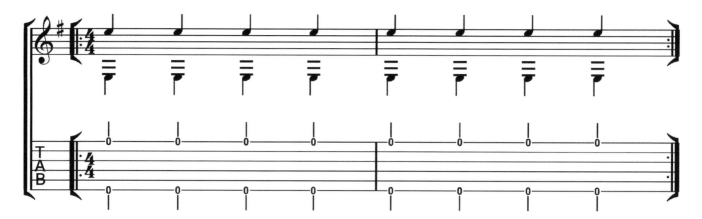

Try repeating the previous example but now alternate between using your ring and middle finger for each pick of the high E string. This may feel strange at first but try to relax into it. As you get more confident, switch your focus to your breathing while you listen to your playing. Are you in time?

Now we will play two 1/8th notes for every bass note. Alternate between using your ring and middle fingers for the high notes before trying to use just one finger.

Example 1c:

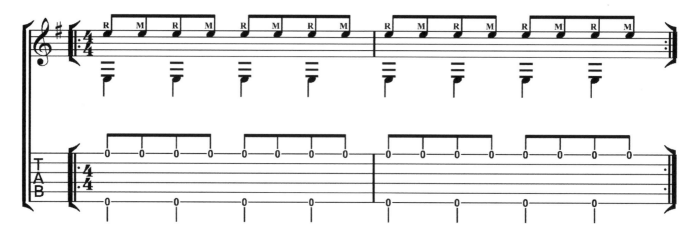

Use a metronome to gradually speed up example 1c to around 100bpm (beats per minute). Try recording yourself playing against the metronome and listen to whether you're in time.

Next we will learn to feel 1/8th note triplets. The following example shows three melody notes for each bass note. Use your ring and middle finger to play the melody notes before introducing the index finger and playing the melody with the ring, middle and index (R, M and I) fingers. Try using this sequence of fingers in reverse too. Concentrate on playing in time and relaxing into the feel. Don't forget to slightly palm mute the bass strings to help differentiate between the steady bass line and the melody notes.

Example 1d:

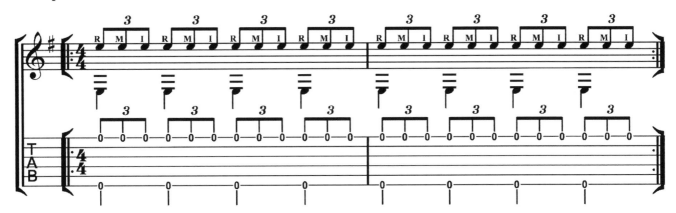

Before adding a more interesting melody, play the following example with four melody notes per beat. Make sure your thumb is consistently in time with the click. Start by using your middle and index fingers on the high notes but experiment with single fingers and other combinations as much as you can.

Example 1e:

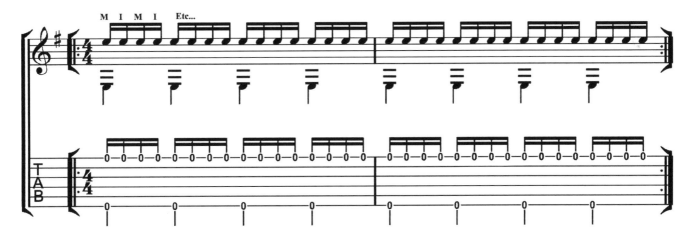

The following examples combine some of the previous rhythms. Work through them and gradually increase the speed of each exercise using a metronome. It's good to increase the metronome speed in increments of about 8 bpm.

Example 1f:

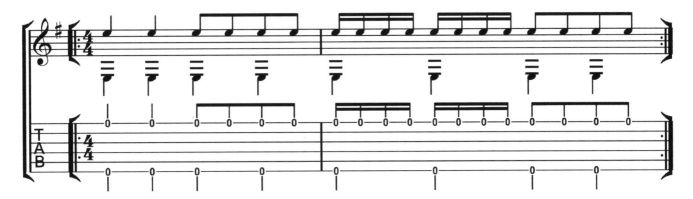

Example 1g:

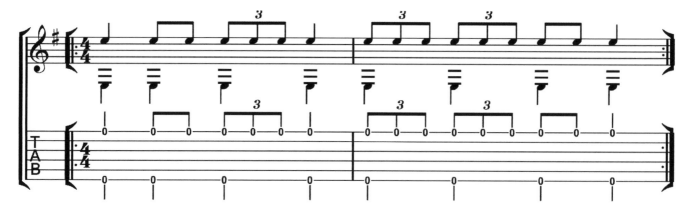

Now we can begin to play more than one pitch for the melody. While this example may look simple on paper, it may begin to stretch your coordination. Pay attention to the fingering in the picking hand. M and R are just a suggestion but whatever fingering you choose, make sure you use an alternate finger when playing two notes on the same string.

You should be able to hear now how these rudimentary exercises are working towards playing authentic blues phrases.

Example 1h:

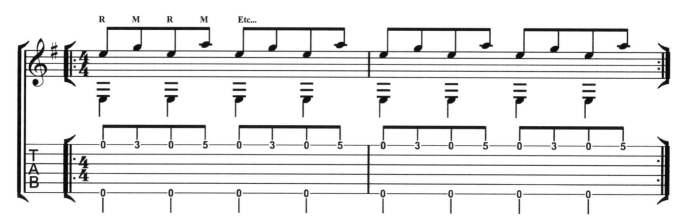

This example uses notes that move across two strings. When changing strings it is O.K. to pick with the same finger twice.

Example 1i:

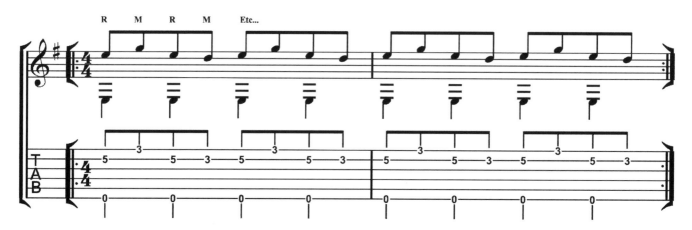

Here's a similar idea that uses a triplet feel. Experiment by using different pairs of fingers in the picking hand. You may find that M and I are fairly comfortable and that M and R need some work. Developing freedom in the picking hand is an important goal, so persevere with these exercises if you find particular combinations challenging. Whatever fingers you decide to use, always alternate your fingers during these exercises and avoid using the same finger twice in a row when playing on the same string.

Example 1j:

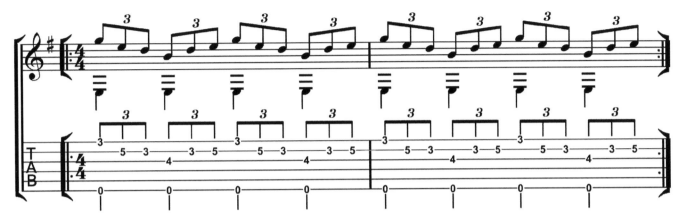

Record your playing and check to see if you're in time. As you gain confidence gradually speed up the metronome. 50bpm is a good starting point and you should gradually try to reach 100bpm over a period of weeks.

In the following example, I have introduced a common bass note figure called an *alternating bass*. Use your picking hand thumb to pick both bass notes and play the fretted note on the 5th string (B) with your second finger. Remember to rest the heel of your picking hand gently on bass strings to keep them slightly muted.

Example 1k:

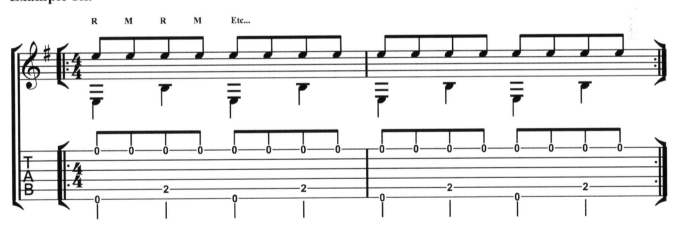

Now we will combine a melody with the bass note pattern.

Example 1l:

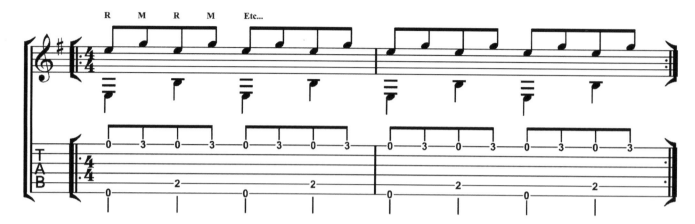

Here's a similar idea with a slightly more challenging melody. Use your little finger to play the fretted melody notes and focus on keeping the bass line smooth and in time.

Example 1m:

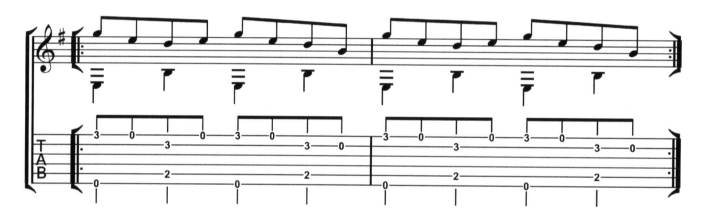

This example builds on example 1m but adds a few faster notes. Keep the bass even and steady.

Example 1n:

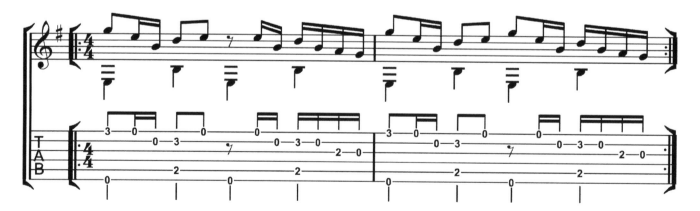

Play through example 1m again, but this time, hold down an E Major or an E7 chord. Even though you're not playing any of the chord notes you're holding, it's essential to learn to hold chords while adding melodies. See if you can figure out how to play example 1n while holding down a chord. A little adjustment is necessary as you play through the melody.

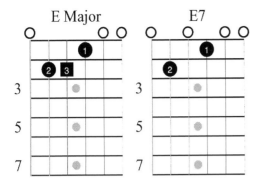

Try varying the melody in example 1m if you can. The most important part of the exercises is to keep the bass line constant and in time while using the thumb.

The next example moves between two chords. E Major and A Major. Begin by playing the example without holding down the chords but when you gain confidence hold down the full chords as you play through the example.

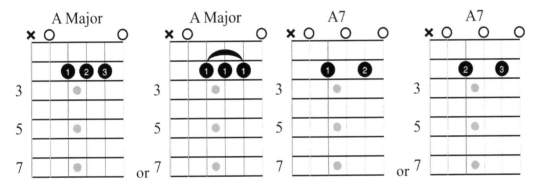

Example 1o:

Now here's a similar idea but the melody is now a little more complex. Notice the 1/8th note rest on the first beat that helps to separate the melody from the bass line.

Example 1p:

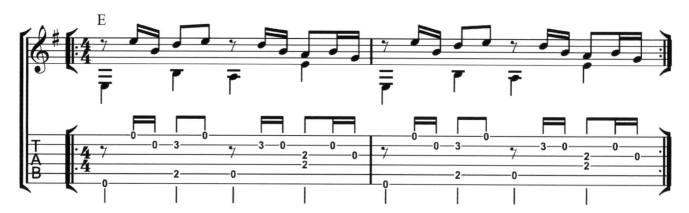

The trickiest thing in example 1p is keeping control of the bass line. Notice that two notes are played in succession on the A string. We will look in much more detail at bass lines later, but for now check out this next example. The melody is the same as before, but I've now added another note into the bass part. Use your second finger to fret the low G note.

Example 1q:

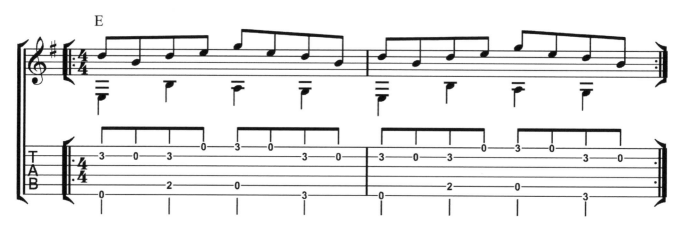

The following exercises are more like traditional licks, but help you to build independence between your thumb and picking fingers. I have simplified the bass line to help you get used to these new rhythms.

You may wish to begin by separating out the melody part and introducing the bass line when you are comfortable. As always the thing to focus on is a constant bass note on each beat. Record yourself if you're not sure whether you are managing to keep the bass consistent.

Listen to the audio example to help you get the feel for these phrases.

The audio files for this book are available at **www.fundamental-changes.com**.

Example 1r:

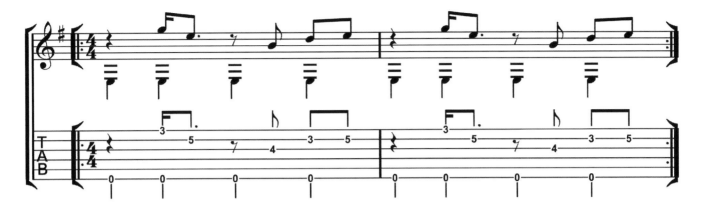

Example 1s:

The next two examples feature off-beat melody notes against an alternating bass line.

Example 1t:

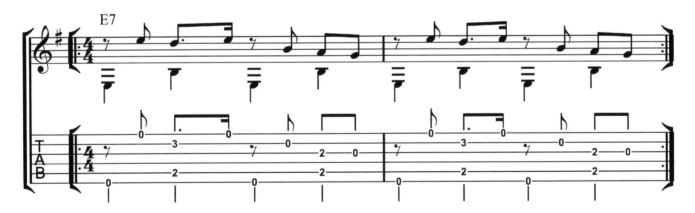

Example 1u:

The following examples reintroduce triplets and some of their quicker subdivisions and combine them with an alternating bass line. Begin by playing the examples *without* holding down the notated chords so that you can get a feel for the music. When you start to gain confidence hold down a full E7 chord and discover how your fingering needs to change to play the same line.

Example 1v:

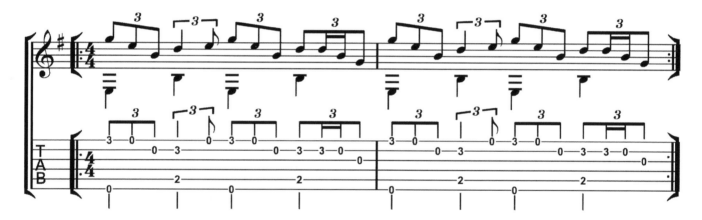

Example 1w:

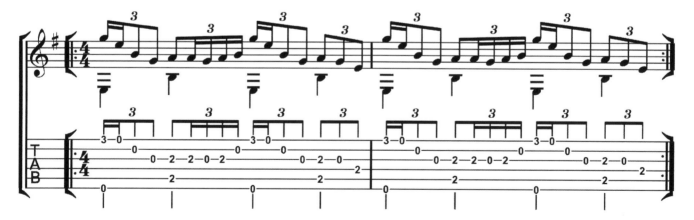

As you become more comfortable with these ideas, you should start experimenting by changing the order of the melody notes and exploring new melodic ideas. All of the notes used so far come from the E Minor Pentatonic scale, which you may already know. We will be looking at this scale in much greater detail in the next chapter when we build our soloing skills.

It is essential that you keep your foot tapping on the beat and concentrate on making sure your thumb stays in time whether you are playing just a single note bass line or using the alternating bass technique.

Any of the above ideas can be adapted to be played over the E major to A Major bass line we studied in example 1p, so again, it's worth experimenting with melodies over these bass lines.

One piece of advice that I took from Joe Pass a long time ago was that *the bass line is always your most important concern*. The bass provides a rhythmic foundation for the listener and 'frames' every melody note that you play. If the bass starts to get shaky then the whole structure will quickly collapse. To build a strong, consistent bass line, practice very slowly and think about how any fretted bass notes need to coordinate with the melodic phrase. Gradually speed up and you will find that the fingers naturally start to move together.

This first chapter has really been about *programming* your fingers and developing coordination. Speed is a distant concern so always make sure your head is in control of what you're playing, not your hands.

In the next chapter, we explore specific soloing ideas and map out some important scale shapes you should know.

Chapter Two: Introducing Scales and Soloing

You may have noticed that in the last chapter most of the melodic phrases were based around just a few notes. These notes were all contained in the scale of *E Minor Pentatonic*. The notes of this scale can be played in two different positions near the bottom of the guitar.

The first position of the E minor Pentatonic Scale uses open strings.

Example 2a:

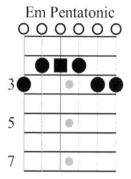

As most of the time we will be busy on the lower strings, the top three or four strings of this scale will be most useful to use when soloing. Try playing down the scale again, but this time add a 1/4 note bass line on the low E string.

Example 2b:

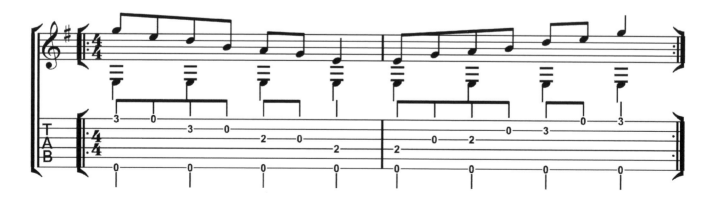

We will begin by looking at some useful licks using this scale shape and see how we can use embellishments and techniques to move from playing boring scales to interesting, musical *phrases*. Each example is played as an isolated 'lick' and is then played with a 1/4 note bass line.

As a quick aside, it's important to remember that music doesn't come from scales. Scales come from music. In the beginning there was just melody, it wasn't until later that musicologists came along and organised these wild, beautiful melodies into groups of tame notes called scales that could then be 'formalised' and taught to others. While scales are a convenient way to communicate an idea, don't get stuck thinking that these are the only notes you can play.

Bends

The first lick in this section introduces the concept of the blues bend or *curl*. The curl is a tiny microtonal (less than a semitone) bend on a note to give it more musical expression and power. They can be played anywhere, but they are much more common on certain pitches. Bends can be played slowly or quickly and can be manipulated while they're being sounded. Listen carefully to the audio tracks provided and carefully copy the phrasing of each bend. Notice that this curl doesn't return to its original pitch, instead the melody jumps directly to the open string

Example 2c:

The following example introduces a different kind of bend and also a *pull-off*. We will look at pull-offs in more detail later so let's focus on the bend for now. The bend on the 3rd string is a very quick sharpening of the note A before returning immediately to the original pitch. The note is then pulled-off to the open third (G) string. Listen carefully to how this lick is played on the audio track.

Example 2d:

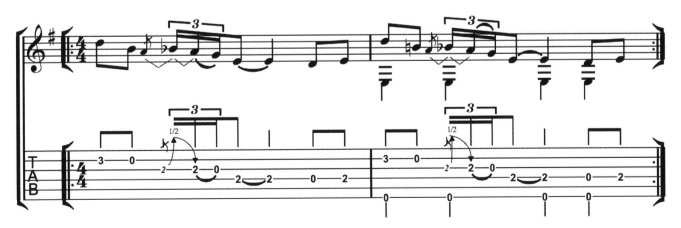

Example 2e combines both of the previous bends into one phrase.

Example 2e:

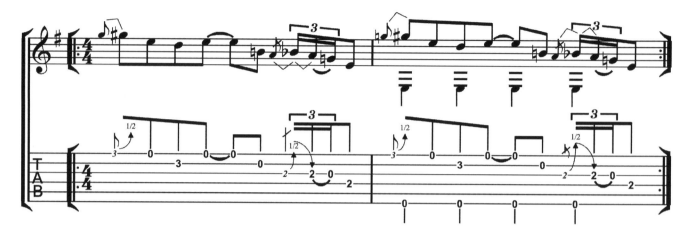

The following lick uses the same bend on the first (E) string, but the bend is much slower lasting for a full beat.

Example 2f:

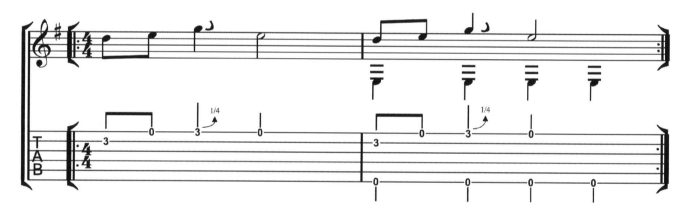

The next example shows how you can use bends of different lengths on the same note to develop a lick from just a few notes.

The note A is bend up a full tone to the 5th of the scale (B) twice. The first time the bend is played quickly and the second time the bend takes two beats to complete. Use your second finger to bend the G string and support it by playing the first finger behind it on the string. Bends this low down on the guitar can take practice and patience to master as you may need to build more strength.

Don't forget the last bass note in the second bar!

Example 2g:

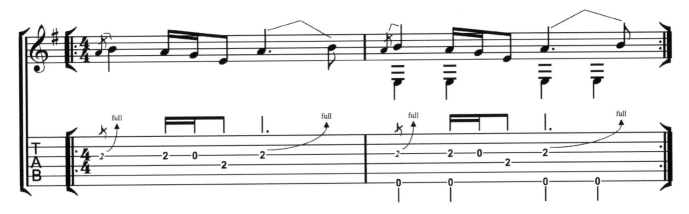

The next bend to master is the *prebend*. Prebends can be quite tricky at first, especially when combined with the 1/4 note bass line.

The idea when prebending (as the name suggests) is to bend the note to pitch *before* striking it. This skill will take time to master because you don't have any aural reference as to how far to bend. Keep practicing and you will begin to feel how far the string needs to be bent to target the correct pitch.

In the next example, the note D is bent up to the root (E) before striking it. Again, support the bend with spare fingers and listen carefully to the pitch when you pick the note. You'll quickly know if it's not right.

Example 2h:

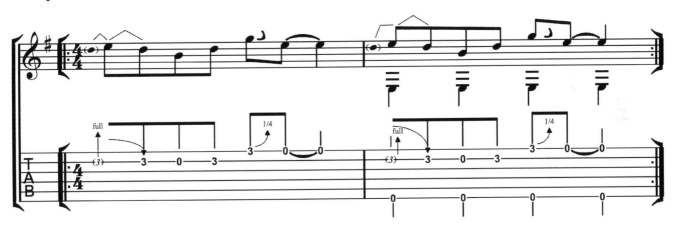

When playing any kind of blues guitar lick, it is normal for notes to be bent a tiny amount all the time, even when the bend isn't notated. By adding curls and other tiny manipulations to each note, guitarists can add an enormous amount of expression to their phrases. If you listen carefully to any good blues guitar solo, you will hear that almost every note has some kind of bend, slide, vibrato or other subtle technique added to create a more vocal, fluid line that mimics the human voice.

Jeff Beck is one such master of subtle note manipulation, and you should check out anything by him to hear tasteful, musical use of any technique in this book.

In the next section we will explore notes slightly higher up the neck and introduce slides into our playing while continuing to learn acoustic blues guitar vocabulary and technique.

Second Position Soloing, Slides and Double-stops

Let's now move up the neck a little bit and explore the second position of the E Minor Pentatonic scale. It can be played on the guitar in the following way.

Example 2i:

Em Pentatonic

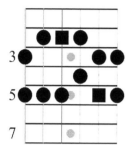

Memorise this pattern by playing through the scale slowly with a metronome, and gradually increasing the speed. Once you are confident, play through the notes on the top four strings while keeping a steady low E bass note.

Example 2j:

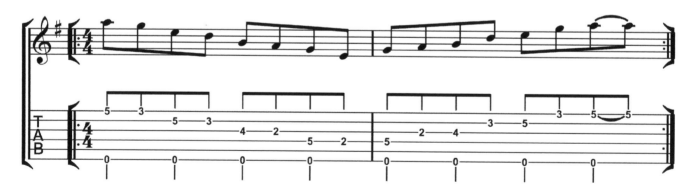

There are a few very useful notes in this scale that can be bent and these are demonstrated in the following licks. Remember you should experiment with how quickly and how far you bend each note.

Example 2k:

Example 2l:

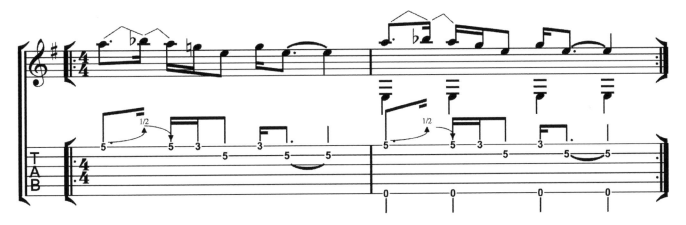

The bend in the following example will be quite challenging at first, as you need to bend one and a half tones from the root note (E) to the b3rd (G). In fact, if you are playing an acoustic guitar then you should avoid this example all together. Use your third finger to bend the note and support it by placing the first and second fingers behind it on the string.

Also notice that the bend is *choked* by a palm mute in the picking hand. You don't need to worry about this at first, but it's a great technique to add in when you develop some confidence with the bend.

As always, master the lick in the first bar before adding in the bass notes in the second bar.

Example 2m:

As you can see and hear in example 2k, I have notated a *slide* into the final note of the bar (E). Slides can be played in two main ways.

Firstly, a note that is being slid up to another can have no rhythmic value. These slides are called *glissandos (gliss)* and create a human, vocal effect that enhances the melody. It does not normally matter where these slides begin so long as you end up at the target pitch at the right time. However, sliding a short distance into a target note creates a different feel than sliding a long distance.

Use the notated glissandos to embellish the melodies in the following phrases. Listen to the audio examples to hear how they should be played. Start by sliding from the indicated pitch (in brackets), but as your skills develop try sliding longer or shorter distances and try varying the speed at which you slide. You do however need to be careful to reach the target note at the right time.

Example 2n:

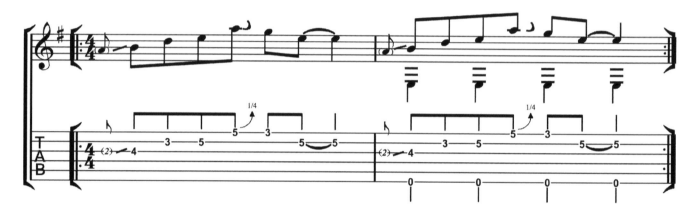

Example 2o:

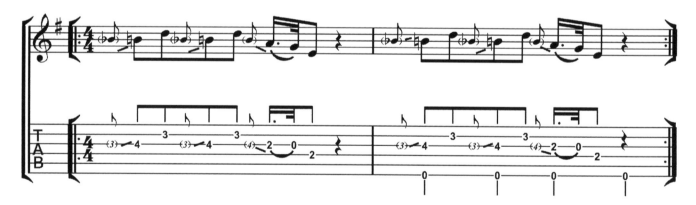

The other type of slide is played when the rhythmic value of the starting note has been completed. These slides are a smooth way of linking the notes of a phrase together or changing position on the guitar.

In the following examples, be careful to hold each pitch for its full duration, and then slide smoothly and cleanly into the following note. You can also experiment by re-picking the note as you slide it, or sliding it without the extra strike.

Example 2p:

Example 2q:

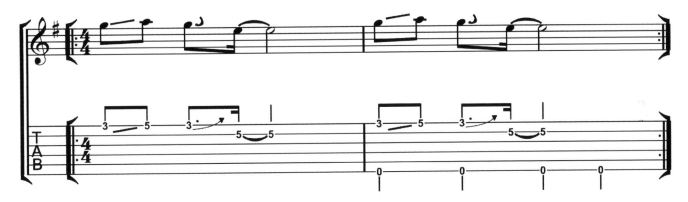

Compare example 2n with example 2p. The first slide in each example looks similar but sounds very different.

The next example combines both slides and grace notes in a new phrase. Notice that I have written a grace note slide from *above* the target pitch. This technique can take a bit of getting used to, so isolate and learn the lick in the first bar before playing it with the 1/4 note bass line.

Example 2r:

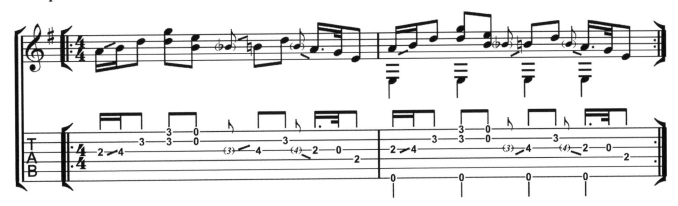

Example 2r also introduces a technique called a *double-stop* where two notes are played together. Double-stops are an extremely useful musical device, especially when playing the guitar unaccompanied as they allow us to combine solo lines with a more 'chordy' texture. The following examples show you how to incorporate some important double-stops into your playing with the first two Minor Pentatonic positions.

Example 2s combines grace note slides with a curl on the top string to create a phrase that could easily be used as an accompaniment riff.

Example 2s:

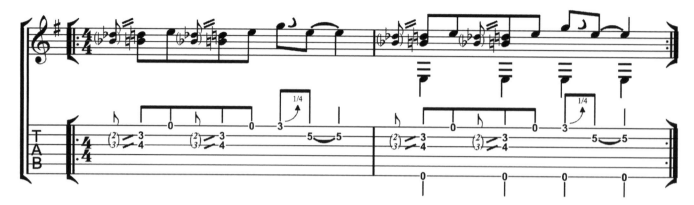

Use your first finger to play the initial double-stop bend. When a starting point isn't specified for a slide you can experiment with where you begin the movement. Use your second and third fingers to slide into the double-stop in beat four. This lick contains a note that isn't in the E Minor Pentatonic scale (C#), and it is bend up towards the D on the second string.

Example 2t:

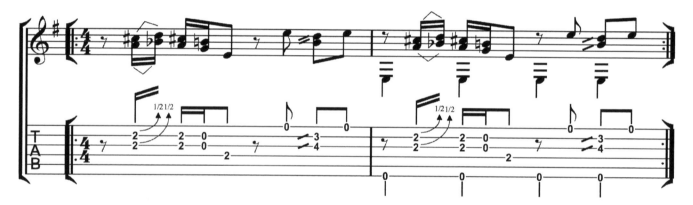

Example 2u may be a little bit challenging at first. You have to play a curl on the top G (beat two) while letting the open second (B) string ring out. By only bending the top G a tiny amount you will create an authentic blues sound and avoid accidentally muting the B string.

Example 2u:

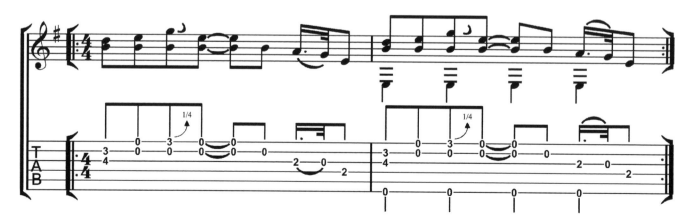

In Example 2v, a sliding double-stop is followed by a pull-off onto the open strings. Again, experiment with the slide into beat four. I would suggest that a one-fret slide is a good starting point. The slide in beat two is quite quick, so listen to the audio example to hear how this lick should sound. Make sure you isolate the lick in bar one before introducing the 1/4 note bass pattern in bar two.

Example 2v:

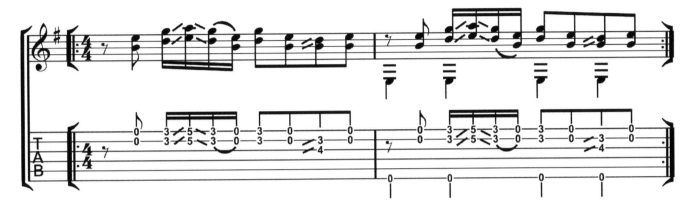

We will explore further up the neck later, but the following example shows how we can use the same idea in two places on the guitar. Use your first and second fingers to play these double-stops, and give a slight curl to the note on the lower string. Make sure that you don't accidentally bend the note on the higher string too. The bend at the 8th fret is a very common idea in acoustic blues guitar and has been played by almost every guitarist of this style. It's affectionately known as a *train whistle* bend.

Example 2w:

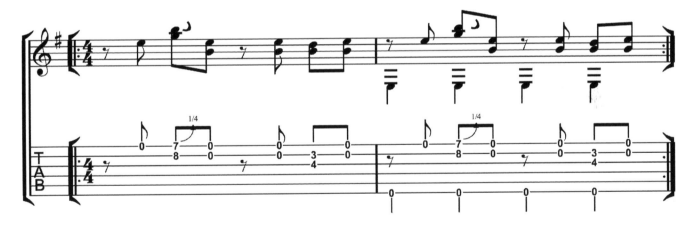

The next double-stop bend is quite challenging, and it will probably take some time before you develop the strength and control needed to execute it properly. Hold the second string down with your third finger and use your second finger to play a slight bend on the third string.

This is a very short, isolated phrase but as your fluency develops you will easily start to combine it with other open string licks to fill out the rest of the bar.

Example 2x:

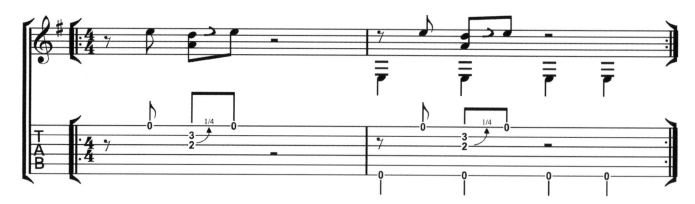

The next example combines a double-stop bend with a sustained *pedal* tone on the top string. A pedal tone is normally a repeated note in the bass (like you are playing on the open sixth string) but pedal notes can also be above the moving melody.

Hold the top note (G) steady with your third finger while playing the bends on the third string with your second finger. In your picking hand, try using your ring and index finger to play the double-stops.

Example 2y:

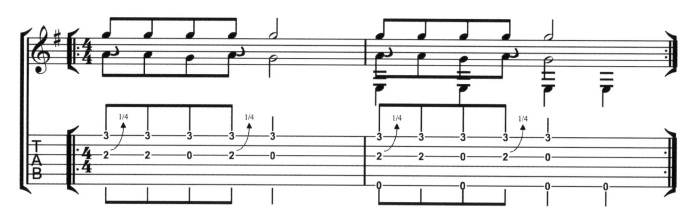

Any note on the guitar can easily be played an octave higher by playing it twelve frets above. In other words, the open string notes of the guitar are repeated at the 12th fret. The first position of the E Minor Pentatonic scale can, therefore, be played without open strings and one octave higher in the following way:

Em Pentatonic

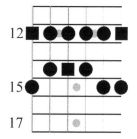

Notice that this shape is identical to the first position of the Minor Pentatonic scale but doesn't use any open strings.

This means that we can move any of our open string blues licks up by twelve frets, and then play the line an octave higher provided we are willing to re-finger it.

For example, we could easily move example 2t up an octave and play it in the following way:

Example 2z:

Notice how the first open E is now played on the 12th fret of the first string, but I had to re-finger the second open E on the 17th fret to make it easier to reach.

I encourage you to experiment with the first position of E Minor Pentatonic scale played at the 12th fret. This is the most commonly used scale shape by guitarists and it is also movable like a barre chord. Any lick can easily be transposed up and down the guitar neck into different keys by simply moving the scale shape into a new location.

For example, you can play an A Minor Pentatonic scale like this:

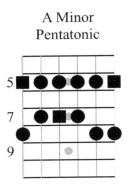

The root note (A) can be played on the open A string so it is easy to move all of your first position licks into the key of A Minor.

Chapter Three: Legato and Vibrato

We briefly touched on *pull-offs* in the previous chapter, but now we will take a more detailed look at this important technique and also introduce *hammer-ons*.

Hammer-ons and pull-offs are both categorised as *legato* techniques on the guitar. Although legato is really just the Italian word for smooth, it's possible to really dig in on both of these techniques so they don't sound smooth at all!

To perform a pull-off, pick the first fretted note as normal and then, without re-picking the note, make a firm movement with the fretting finger down towards the floor to sound a note below. Pull-offs can be played onto lower fretted notes or onto open strings, as you will see in the following examples. Think of the fretting finger as an extra pick (plectrum).

Isolate the exercises in the first bar of each example before adding the bass with your thumb. Aim at first to make the pull-off note as loud as possible to increase your strength, but as you gain confidence try to make both notes in each pair equally loud.

You will notice that when you add the 1/4 note bass line, the coordination to pull-off (especially to open strings) will disappear slightly. Stay focused and play each note in time.

Example 3a:

Here's a similar example using the second position of E Minor Pentatonic.

Example 3b:

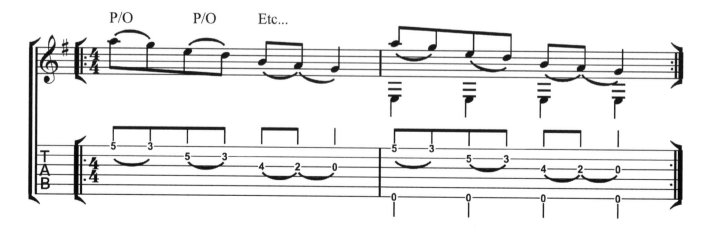

Work towards making each note rhythmically even. It is easy to rush these phrases.

The next exercise is one of the most challenging, yet most important in this book and will test your coordination and left hand / right hand independence. It can be very difficult to pull-off to a lower note if the lower note is on the beat, while keeping the 1/4 note bass consistent with your thumb. Essentially you are picking with your thumb while pulling off with your fretting hand. There is normally an overwhelming desire to repeat the bass note and play it at the wrong time.

Play slowly and carefully through the following example making sure you follow the picking directions. Pick only the first two notes before pulling off to each lower note of each pair and then picking the higher one.

Example 3c:

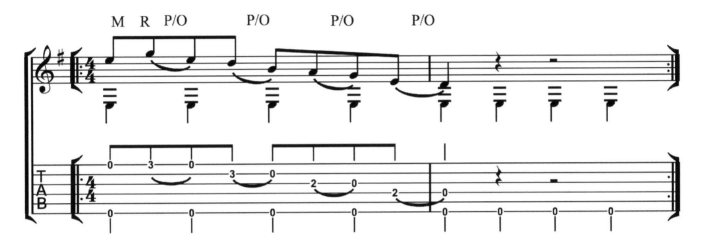

Here's a similar example using the second position of E Minor Pentatonic.

Example 3d:

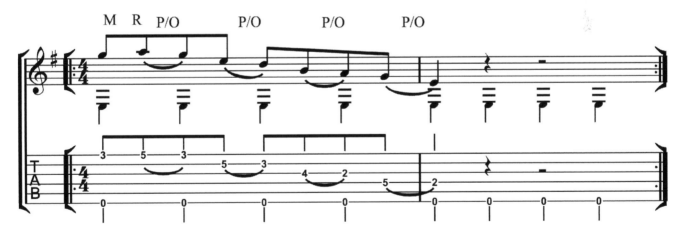

These two exercises were some that really helped my coordination, fluency, and freedom when learning this style.

Hammer-ons are the opposite of pull-offs in that we move from a lower note to a higher one by hammering down a fretting finger without picking the string again. Hammer-ons can be more challenging than pull-offs at first because they need more strength, control, and coordination to execute cleanly and evenly.

To perform a hammer-on, pick the first note normally and use a fretting hand finger to 'slap' or hammer down onto the desired fret above. Be accurate so as not to catch the surrounding strings and make sure the rhythm between the two notes is as even as playing picked notes.

The following examples show you how to hammer-on from open strings and fretted notes. Listen carefully to the audio to hear how evenly each pair of notes is played.

Example 3e:

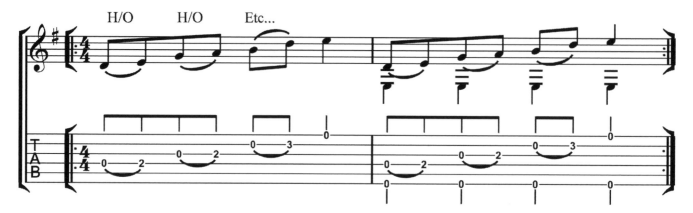

Example 3f:

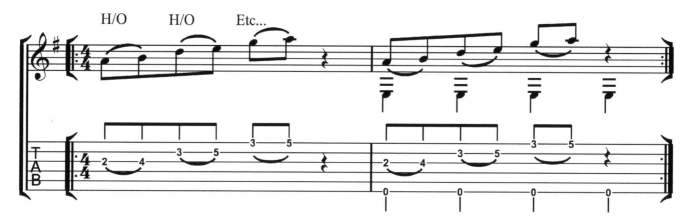

It is again trickier to play a hammer-on from an off-beat to an on-beat with a constant 1/4 note thumbed bass although most people find hammer-ons slightly easier than pull-offs. The following two exercises are a good start to help you develop coordination and fluency.

As with examples 3c and 3d, be careful to follow the picking directions. Only pick the first two notes before hammering on for the first time, and then only pick the first note of each pair.

Example 3g: (Pick where notated with whichever finger is comfortable).

Example 3h:

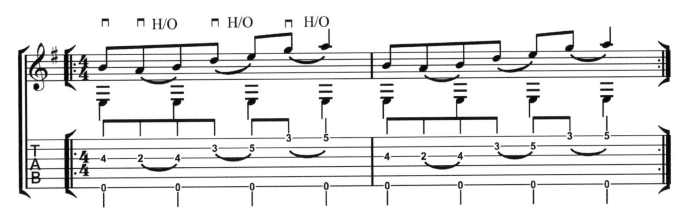

The following example combines hammer-ons with pull-offs and a regular bass note to help you move between different rhythmic placements of the legato techniques. I advise you to go very slowly with these two exercises and focus heavily on rhythmic evenness between each note. Following the picking / articulation directions carefully and you will notice a shift between the two rhythmic placements demonstrated above.

Example 3i:

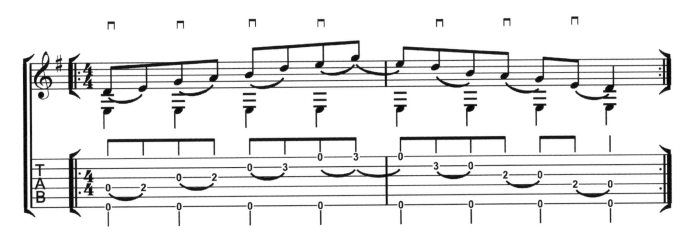

Example 3j:

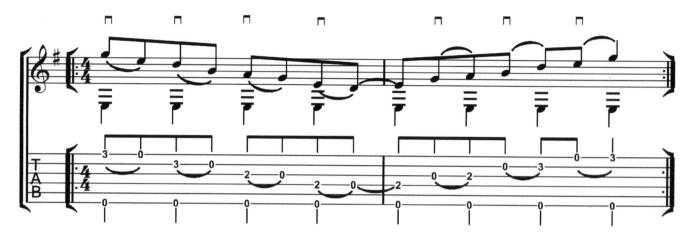

Work through these exercises in the second position, as shown in the previous examples.

Example 3c, 3d, 3g, 3h, 3i and 3j were designed to build the coordination and independence in your right and left hand. If you can master these six exercises you will find that almost any future example, whether picked or legato, is much easier to play. Take a few days or weeks to work on the legato control exercises above, and gradually try to speed them up. Remember though; consistent rhythm and volume is a much more important goal than speed.

As you develop your skills with legato, it's time to use these techniques in new blues vocabulary and combine them with the slides and bends we have already looked at.

Try the following examples. First isolate and memorise the phrase in the first bar before adding the bass line in the second.

Example 3k:

Example 3l:

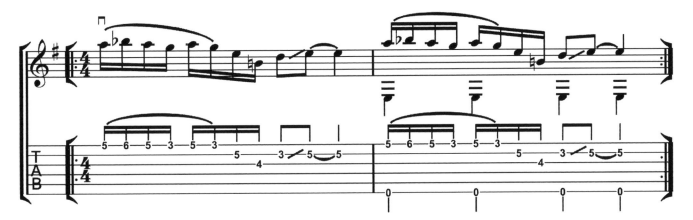

Example 3m:

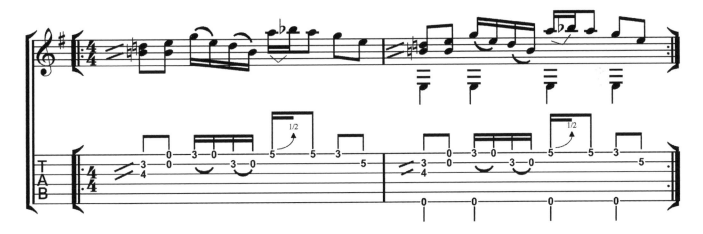

Example 3n:

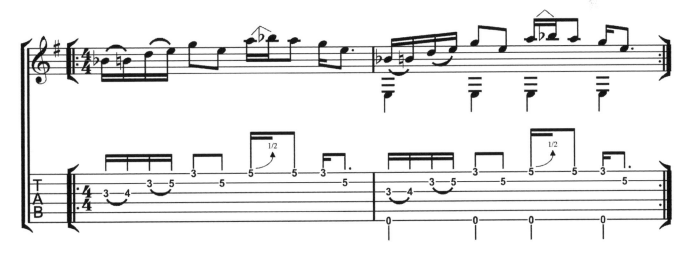

Just as with bends, hammer-ons and pull-offs can be played as grace notes. When playing these lines with the 1/4 note bass figure it may take some time to develop the control to play the grace note very slightly before the bass note.

The following examples show a few common ways to incorporate grace note legato ideas into your lines.

Example 3o:

Example 3p:

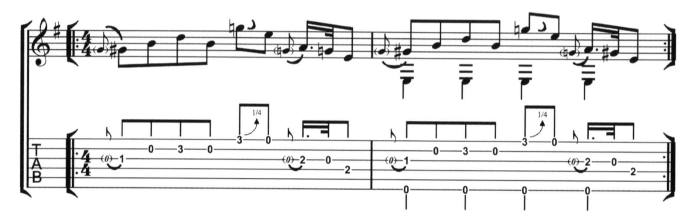

Example 3q:

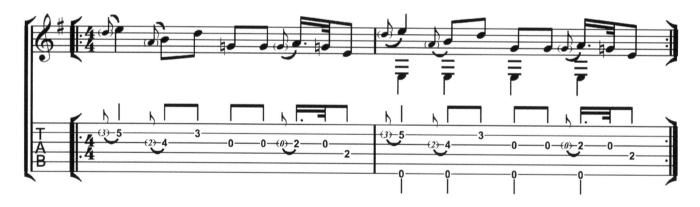

Vibrato

Vibrato is the technique of wavering the pitch of a note by wobbling the fretting finger after the note has been struck. It is one of the most expressive techniques to use on the guitar because it replicates the emotion of the human voice. Vibrato can be used in a variety of different ways, but in early blues guitar it was added to the ends of phrases to enhance the tone and *sustain* of the thin-sounding guitar.

Vibrato is created by slightly rotating the fretting hand so that the first joint (knuckle) of the first finger pushes up against the bottom of the fretboard. This contact creates a pivot that you can use to quickly move the string from side to side. When performing vibrato, the fingers that fret the chosen note should be locked in place so that only the wrist and palm are moving forward and back in the same direction as the guitar neck.

Begin by listening to the difference between the same phrase played with, and without vibrato.

Example 3r:

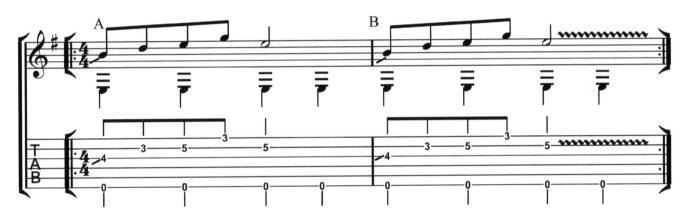

As you can hear, the same phrase played with vibrato has a much more vocal, expressive quality to it.

You should practice adding vibrato with all four fingers of the fretting hand, for example, try the same phrase again, but slide into the final note with your first finger and adding vibrato. Try sliding in with each finger in turn and then adding vibrato.

You can go back through this book and add vibrato to any note in each lick. It's particularly effective at the end of a phrase, but it can be applied on any note in the phrase, especially the longer notes.

You will find that it is a little tricky to keep the 1/4 note bass going when adding vibrato at first, especially when the phrase ends on an off-beat ('and'). For example, the following line ends on the 'and' of beat three and you need to focus on the picking thumb to keep it in time.

Example 3s:

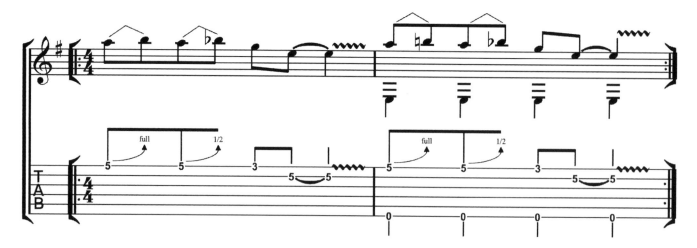

You should also experiment by delaying the point at which you begin to add vibrato to a sustained note, as you don't have to begin immediately. You can create a very dynamic effect by leaving the note to ring unaffected and then gradually introducing the vibrato after a few beats.

Consider too, how *wide* or *fast* you want your vibrato to be. A fast, wide vibrato sounds very different from a slow, narrow vibrato. In the following example, I play just one note and vary the speed and width of the vibrato. This is a great exercise to connect your own expression to your guitar.

Example 3t:

We can also apply vibrato to a double-stop. Play the double-stop in the normal way, turn your wrist so that the index finger is pushing against the underside of the guitar neck and lock your fingers before pivoting your palm.

Be careful to limit the range of your vibrato with double-stops because it is easy to accidently kill the note on the higher string. Listen carefully while you play in order to check that both notes continue to ring.

You may wish to move your index finger away from the bottom of the neck on the higher double-stop to create a more controlled hand position.

Example 3u:

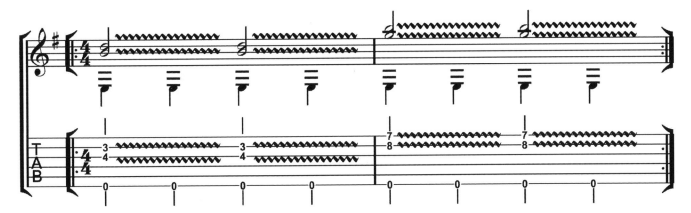

Vibrato is a very personal technique that will continue to develop as long as you play the guitar. If you want more information on how to practice it, check out my book **Complete Technique for Modern Guitar**.

The final examples in this chapter introduce a new position of the E Minor Pentatonic scale which we will be exploring more in later chapters.

Example 3v:

The next examples combine all the techniques we have looked at so far; bends, slides, double-stops, legato and vibrato. By using these techniques you will see how a simple pentatonic phrase can come alive and full of expression.

Example 3w:

Example 3x:

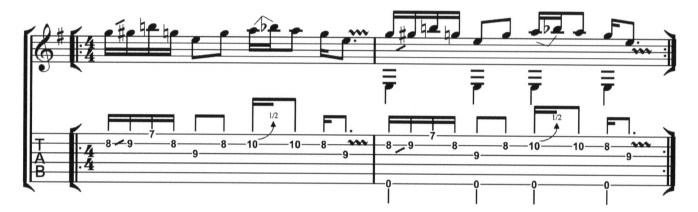

Example 3y:

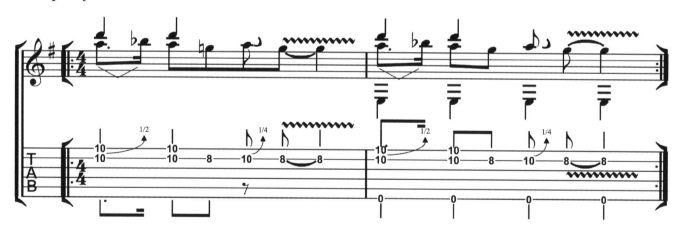

Try coming up with your own licks by blending all of the techniques we've discussed.

In the next chapter, we will look at increasing your rhythmic independence by using *syncopation*.

Chapter Four: Syncopation

Syncopation is 'playing against, or off the beat'. In other words, whenever the melodies we play don't line up with the main pulse, or rhythmic subdivisions of the beat, we are using syncopation.

Normally, syncopation is a natural and simple part of modern music, however, in fingerstyle acoustic blues, syncopation presents a big challenge because our thumb still needs to be playing steady, unsyncopated 1/4 notes. In essence, our thumb is playing on the beat and our picking fingers are playing off the beat.

This level of complexity is obtainable, but it takes some very focused and careful practice. In this chapter, we look at how to master the syncopated playing that forms a large part of fingerstyle blues melodic vocabulary.

We will begin by looking at the most simple forms of syncopation before moving on to more examples. Hopefully, the first example shouldn't be too difficult. The thumb plays constant 1/4 notes and the notes of the E Minor Pentatonic scale are played on every off-beat (between the thumb picks). Keep your foot tapping on the beat and focus on matching the sensation in your foot to the movement of your thumb.

Example 4a:

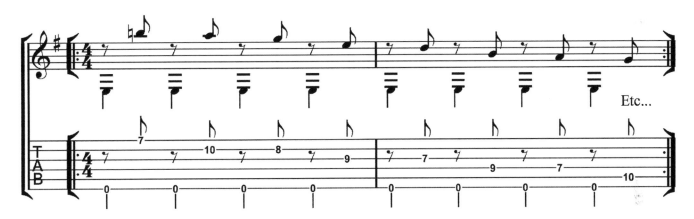

Although each melody note is written as a short 1/8th note for clarity, try to let each note ring for as long as possible. Come up with your own melodic variations based on this rhythm, and spend time exploring different shapes and changing direction. For example, you could play this idea down in position two.

Example 4b:

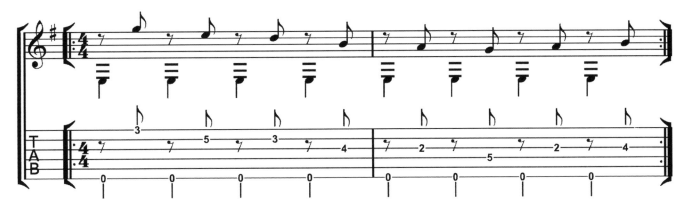

Explore the neck as much as possible using this idea.

The next stage is to make up some licks that are based on this syncopated rhythm. Not every note is played on the off-beat, but that is the general principle behind each line.

Example 4c:

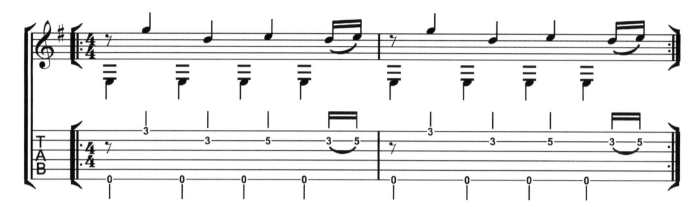

Don't be daunted by the look of the next example, it follows the same general principle as the previous idea, there are just a few quicker notes. Listen to the audio tracks to help you and go slowly. The last beat is a little tricky.

Example 4d:

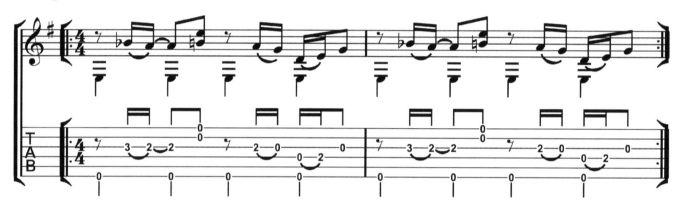

The next example combines an off-beat bend with an off-beat slide.

Example 4e:

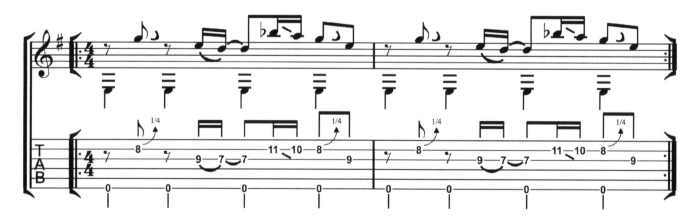

It would be possible to fill this whole book with 1/8th note syncopated licks, and you should spend a lot of time working on developing these ideas as they are common in fingerstyle blues guitar and will help you to develop a great deal of independence between the thumb and fingers of your picking hand.

The next stage is to look at ideas that are displaced by a 1/16th note. These will really challenge your concentration and finger independence so go very slowly when practicing the following examples.

The first example keeps just one note in the melody and allows you to get a feel for this difficult syncopation. Listen to the audio example and make sure you tap your foot on the beat. Once again, focus on your foot and synchronise the feeling of your foot with your thumb pick.

In this example, we displace the 1/8th note melody by a 1/16th, by playing a 1/16th note on the first beat and then continuing in 1/8th notes. This is a great way to sound like you are playing faster than you are and to add intensity to the melody.

Example 4f:

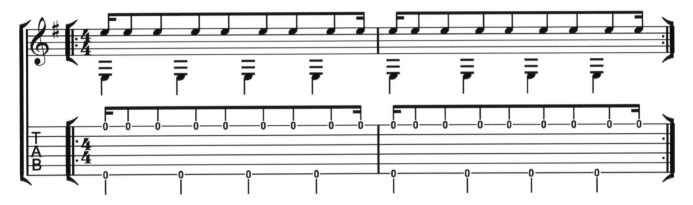

The next example is similar however the first 1/16th note isn't played.

Example 4g:

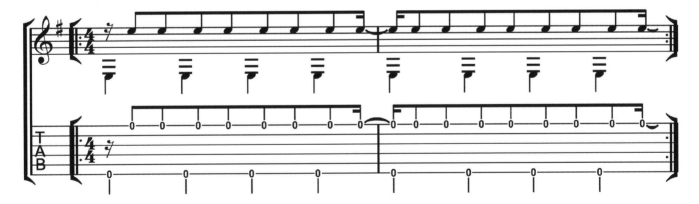

Now try playing an open-position E Minor Pentatonic scale with this rhythm. You may find this quite difficult at first, but that is just your body and mind getting used to the feeling of playing these ideas.

Example 4h:

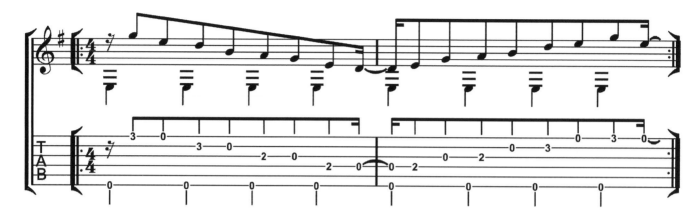

The next few examples demonstrate some licks that are based around this 1/16th note displacement. They are all quite difficult, and it will help if you can count the 1/16th notes out loud "1 2 3 4" across each beat.

In this first example, you place each of the 1/8th notes on the second and fourth 1/16th notes in each beat. Listen carefully to the audio and tap your foot!

Example 4i:

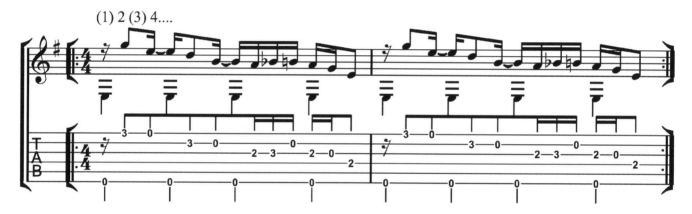

The following example will be very difficult at first so I suggest that you break it down beat by beat.

Count out loud and try to phrase the lick with the audio track. Be very aware of your foot tapping as it will want to move onto the first melody note instead of the beat. This must be avoided at all costs! To develop true independence, your foot must be in charge of keeping time and your thumb must follow.

Tap your foot in double time if you need to, but make sure it is syncing with the bass, not the first bend.

Persevere with this lick, as it will teach you a great deal.

Example 4j:

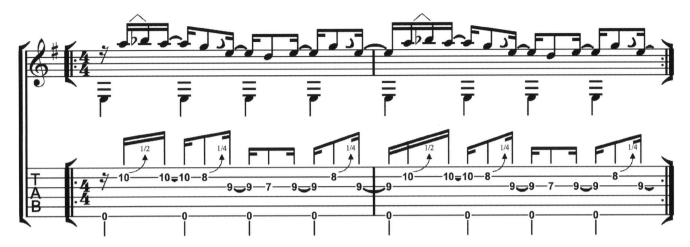

The next line is again quite challenging so listen carefully to the audio and focus on the movement of your foot. While these lines are difficult at first, they will greatly improve the independence in your right and left hands, and between your picking fingers and thumb. Once you have 'broken the back' of these 1/16th note syncopations, you will find that you have much more creative freedom in your melodic lines.

Example 4k:

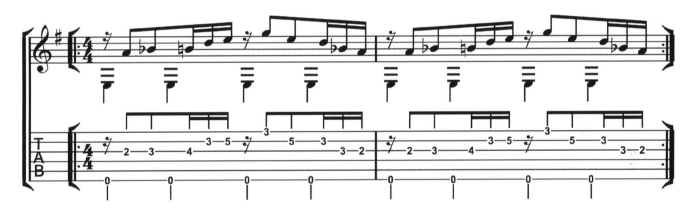

Try to write a few licks yourself using the rhythms of the previous three examples. Gradually begin to add bends, slides and double-stops to enhance the melodies. Add simple embellishments at first and incorporate them very slowly. The next example uses a grace note slide into a double-stop and a curl.

Example 4l:

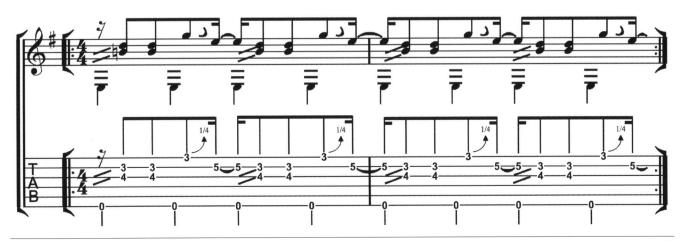

To increase your flexibility and freedom while soloing, it is important to practice moving from unsyncopated to syncopated lines. This is an essential stage in your development that will teach you to incorporate syncopation and note placements unconsciously.

Begin with the following idea that moves from normal to syncopated (off-beat) 1/4 notes.

Example 4m:

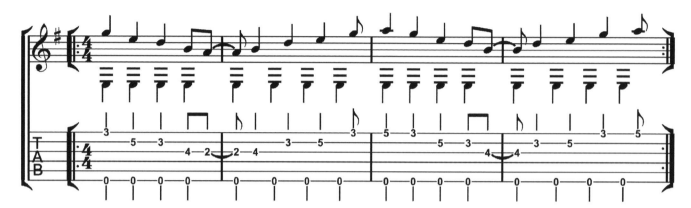

Try playing exercises like this all over the guitar neck; one bar of on-beat melody, and then one bar of off-beat melody.

When you start to get a feel for that, try combining some simple licks together that move from straight playing to syncopation. In the following example I combine example 3k with example 4d:

Example 4n:

This lick could form a great riff to underpin a whole song although you may find a problem area occurs as you begin the repeat. Keep your foot moving!

The next line combines example 3w and 4e:

Example 4o:

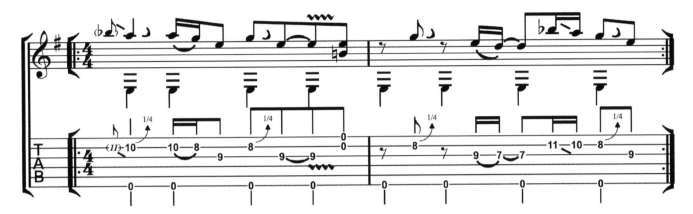

Combine some of the 1/8th note lines with the syncopated ideas you wrote earlier and work on moving seamlessly between them. Gradually increase the amount of time you play for while consciously moving between the two types of line. Eventually you will internalise this feel and it will come out naturally in your playing.

Next, incorporate some 1/16th note syncopations into your playing by combining lines in a similar way. 1/16th notes are harder so be sure to practice diligently in a slow and focused way. The secret to all these rhythms is to keep your foot pounding on the beat.

Begin by working on the following exercise that moves between 1/16th notes on, and off the beat.

Example 4p:

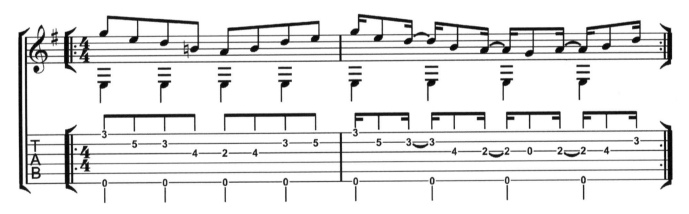

Example 4p is quite taxing at first so try playing along with the audio example. Focus on keeping your thumb and your foot together and try to hear the line as a whole, not just as individual notes. As you gain confidence, gradually increase the speed of your metronome to help build muscle memory.

Now try combining some syncopated and unsyncopated 1/16th note lines so you learn to move freely between the two.

The following line combines examples 3m and 4i:

Example 4q:

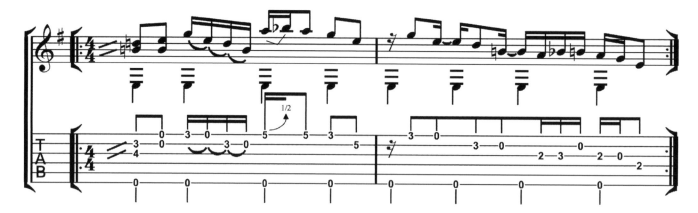

The next line combines example 2l with a new 1/6th note syncopated phrase.

Example 4r:

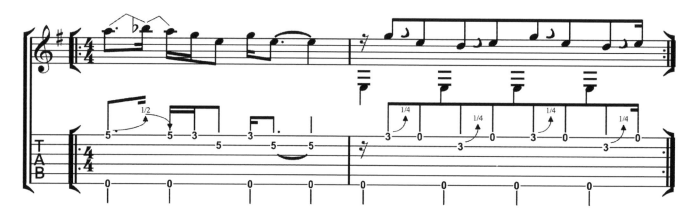

Syncopation is definitely one of the harder techniques to master in fingerstyle blues guitar, or indeed, any kind of music. However, it is also one of the most useful and musical techniques we can work on, because it completely frees up our note *placement* in the bar. When we can pick and choose where we rhythmically place notes in a melody we can be truly expressive. The biggest challenge is keeping the thumb on the beat, but this does become easier with time.

Continue practicing ideas that use this kind of displaced syncopation by writing targeted licks and phrases that use the rhythmic placements above. If a 1/16th note syncopation is difficult to figure out, try tapping your foot in double time (twice as fast), and begin by feeling the line as 1/8th notes, before halving your foot speed and feeling it as 1/16ths again.

If I am struggling with a specific idea, I will always count out the 1/16th notes as "1 2 3 4 1 2 3 4" to ensure I'm placing each note on the correct subdivision of the beat.

In the next chapter, we will look at another common rhythm in fingerstyle blues: triplets.

Chapter Five: Triplet Feel

The triplet feel is an essential part of all blues guitar playing and is created by dividing each beat into three even notes.

This can be written in 4/4 (common time) in the following way:

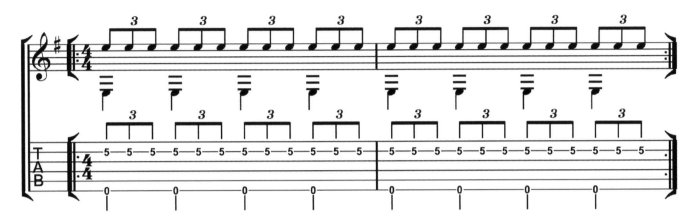

However, it is much tidier to write these lines in the time signature of 12/8 (twelve 1/8th notes per bar that are grouped in threes) to avoid having to write the triplet sign each time:

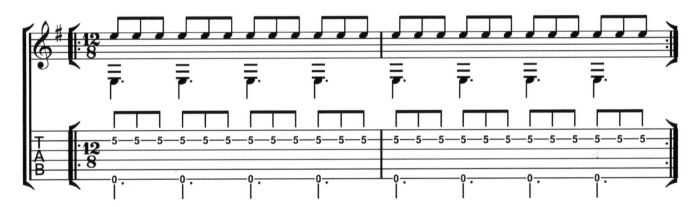

When played at the same tempo, the two previous figures will sound exactly the same.

Begin by playing a minor pentatonic scale ascending and descending using this new triplet rhythm:

Example 5a:

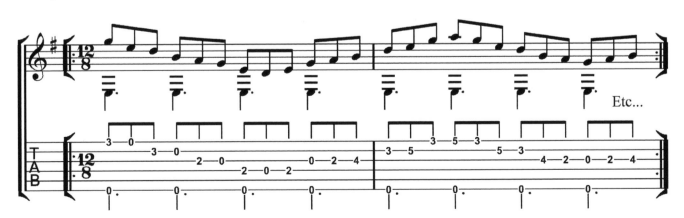

Continue playing pentatonic scale ideas like this all over the neck until you are confident with the triplet rhythmic feel.

We have already looked at the main components of a musical blues vocabulary such as bends, slides, legato vibrato and syncopation, so all that is needed now is to apply these techniques to the triplet rhythm. The difficulty is getting the picking thumb and fingers used to the new feel and developing the same level of independence and control.

The following lines will help you to internalise the triplet feel and teach you a great deal of new vocabulary.

In the first example, pay attention to the grace note slides 'from nowhere'.

Example 5b:

In example 5c, we add a curl and vibrato.

Example 5c:

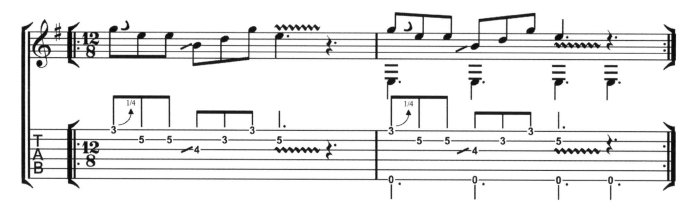

The following example starts with a long, slow bend so be sure to keep the triplet rhythm in your head as you play it. Watch out for the quicker final notes.

Example 5d:

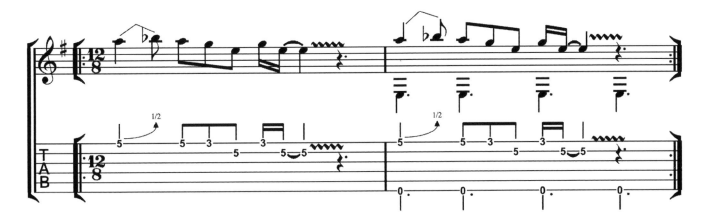

Example 5e begins with a grace note hammer-on before a grace note slide into the B on the third string.

Example 5e:

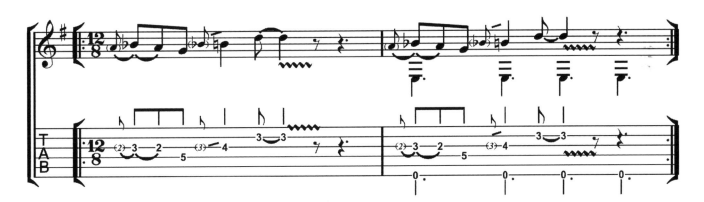

The next example 'doubles up' on the middle note of the second triplet.

Example 5f:

In example 5g we move up the neck and explore the higher range of the guitar. Watch out for the pre-bend on beat three. Play this by holding the previous bend throughout beat two and lowering the pitch at the start of beat three.

Listen to the audio to hear this in action.

Example 5g:

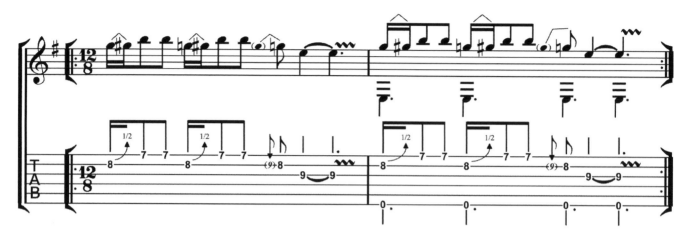

For the next few examples, we will explore another new position of the E Minor Pentatonic scale. Practice it with a 1/4 note bass and with a triplet feel.

Example 5h:

Em Pentatonic

The first example below features upward grace note slides on the first three beats and a downward slide on the last beat of the bar. Let both strings ring and don't be afraid to experiment with the distance of each slide. Watch out for the position shift too!

Example 5i:

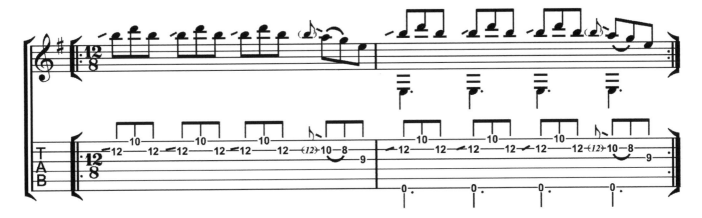

In example 5j, we use the b5 'blue' note (Bb) to add some melodic interest.

Example 5j:

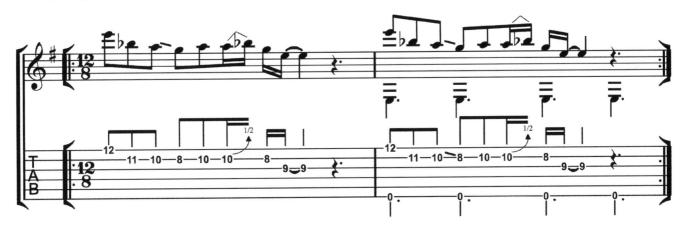

Just as with straight 1/8th notes, we can double up each triplet to play two 1/16th notes on each subdivision of the beat. This idea has been used briefly in a few of the above examples, but the following lines make more use of longer bursts of 1/16th note rhythms.

Be careful of the rhythm: as we are already grouping notes in threes, the 1/16th notes are phrased as three groups of two, not two groups of three. For example:

Example 5k:

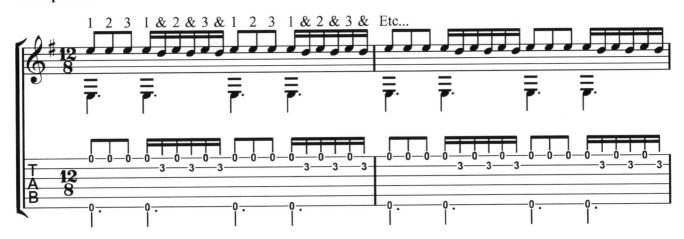

The following lines will help you get the feel for playing longer streams of 1/16th notes in time.

The first example begins with a common ascending blues lick that then quickly descends via the 1/16th note phrases. Watch out for the curl on beat two and the grace note slide on beat three. You may find it easier to transition onto the second finger to play the G on the top string, as it will give you more control when playing the descending phrase.

Example 5l:

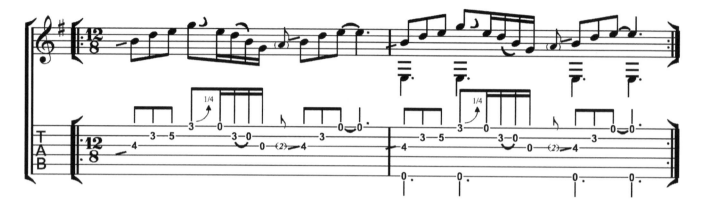

The next example begins with a blues note and uses legato and a slide to smoothly articulate the phrase.

Example 5m:

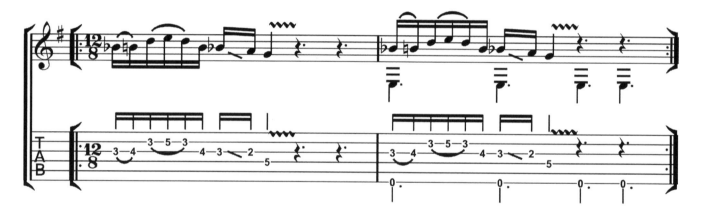

The following idea might be a little challenging at first as it moves between two positions of the E Minor Pentatonic scale. Be sure to slide in hard to the first of each six-note grouping and let each note ring into the next one. By being aggressive with each slide you will help to articulate and define the groupings.

Example 5n:

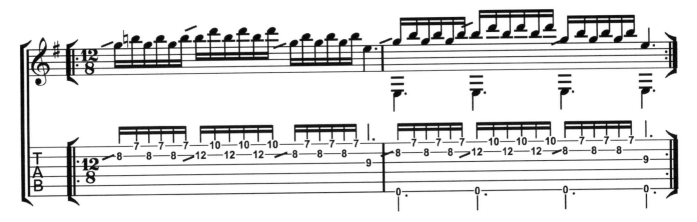

Finally, here is another phrase that teaches you to change position on the guitar neck. The transition from the bend to the pull-offs in beat two may require some special attention. Always master the lick in bar one before adding the bass line in bar two.

Example 5o:

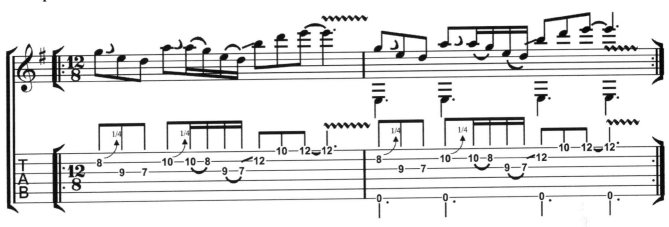

As with all the examples in this book, the rhythm and drive comes from your thumb and foot working in tandem so when you're working on your own faster licks make sure you slow them right down and be very aware of the coordination between the melody and the bass.

In the next chapter, we will look at a new scale, and how to use it to solo over different chords.

Chapter Six: The Major Pentatonic Scale

So far, this book has been focused on building solos over the chords of E Major or E Minor using the Minor Pentatonic scale with the addition of a few 'blue' notes. There are however other scales that can be used to form melodies over an 'E' chord.

The *Major* Pentatonic scale has a bright, uplifting feel, and is a common choice in fingerstyle blues guitar. However its happy-sounding vibe is often too bright to use on the tonic chord of a blues. In fact, most of the 'bluesiness' we hear is created by playing a *minor* scale over a *major* chord. For example, the E *Minor* Pentatonic scale over an E *Major* or E7 chord.

While E Minor Pentatonic works well over an E Major (or E7) chord, E Major Pentatonic doesn't sound very good over an E Minor chord.

Instead of looking at the scale of E Major Pentatonic we will now study the scale of A Major Pentatonic as it is a common choice when playing over the A chord in a blues in the key of E.

We will look at chords and structures more in Chapter Seven but for now, take a quick look at a standard eight-bar blues progression in E.[1]

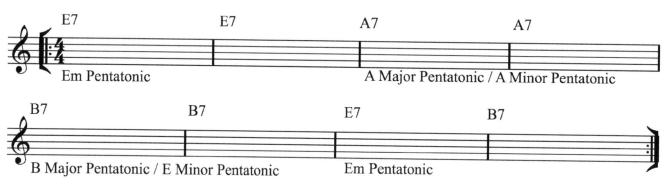

Underneath each chord, I have written some common scale choices for soloing on each chord.

As you can see, the first common use for a Major Pentatonic scale is over the A chord in bar three so let's look at some important Major Pentatonic vocabulary. First begin by learning the A Major Pentatonic scale.

As we can use the open A string as a root note it is possible to play a 1/4 note bass line while playing the A Major Pentatonic Scale.

---

[1] There are many different types of blues structures, including the most common twelve-bar blues. However, many early acoustic blues songs were not based around these structures, with the formalised twelve-bar blues being a later innovation.

Example 6a:

A Maj Pentatonic

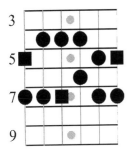

The most important thing to understand is that whenever we play or hear Major Pentatonic lines in the blues, they are normally combined with the Minor Pentatonic scale of the same root. For example, you will freely hear A Major, and A Minor Pentatonic scales together to slightly darken the Major Pentatonic sound and turn it bluesy.

Compare the differences between the A Major and A Minor Pentatonic scales. We will highlight these differences in our melodies to create authentic blues lines.

A Maj Pentatonic   Am Pentatonic

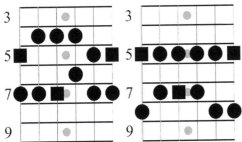

The following lines make use of all the techniques used so far in this book but are now based around the scale of A Major Pentatonic. However, you will notice little hints of the Minor Pentatonic scale tempering the brightness of the Major Pentatonic sound.

Example 6b:

Example 6c:

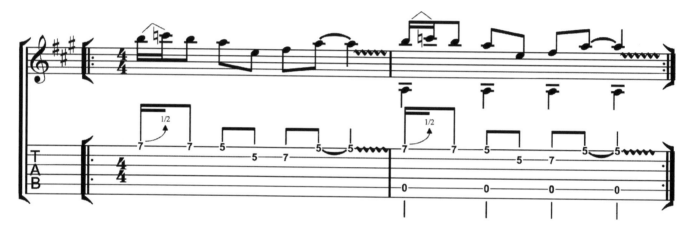

Example 6d:

Example 6e:

Example 6f:

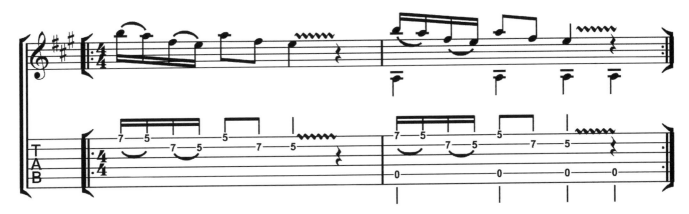

Of course, you should learn and write some lines in 12/8 as well!

Example 6g:

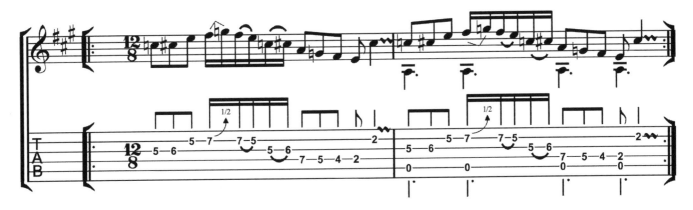

Example 6h:

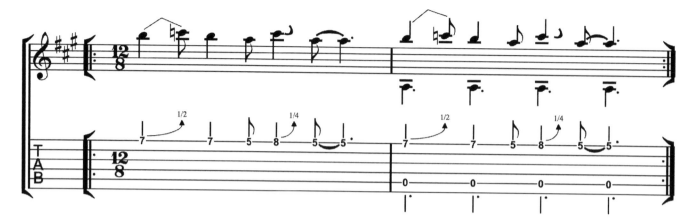

Explore the other shapes of the A Major Pentatonic scale and combine them with the A Minor Pentatonic to form your own blues licks. The following shapes are a great place to start:

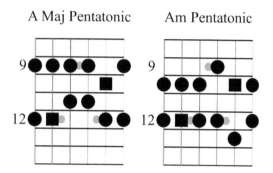

Movable Shapes

One of the great things about the guitar is that if we are playing a scale with no open strings, then we can move it up and down the guitar like a barre chord to access different keys and chords.

When the chord becomes B7 in a blues, we can simply shift all our A Major Pentatonic scale licks up by a tone (two frets) to make the same licks work over the new chord. You could, of course, revert back to playing E Minor Pentatonic ideas on the B7 chord as shown in the diagram at the start of this chapter, but we have already covered these ideas in great detail.

To begin, play an A Major Pentatonic idea from above and then move it up by two frets to turn it into a B Major Pentatonic idea. Eventually you will lose the distinction between Major and Minor Pentatonic lines, and start to view each idea simply as an 'A' lick, a 'B' lick or an 'E' lick.

Example 6i:

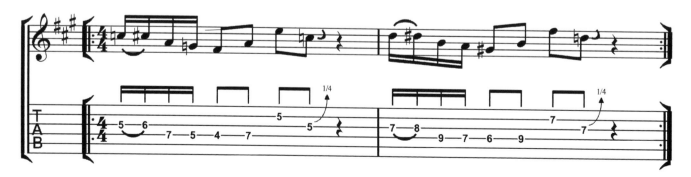

Example 6j:

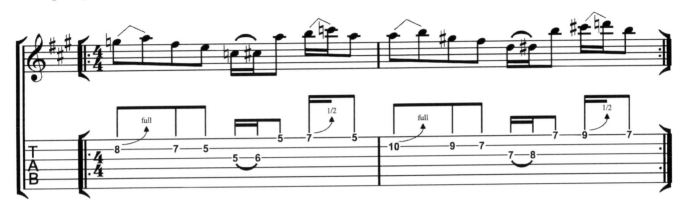

If the lick is quite simple, it can be easy to hold down a B bass note at the 7th fret to continue the bass movement through the chord change. Often this is achieved with a barre across the strings at the 7th fret:

Example 6k:

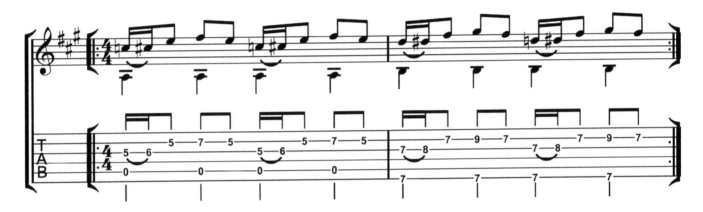

Example 6l:

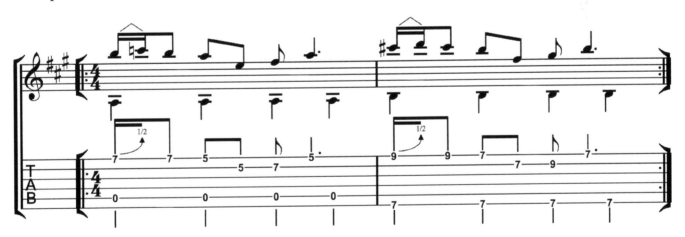

After building a great deal of finger independence, coordination and technique by learning licks and vocabulary, the second section of this book will now examine how to build and play the intricate rhythm and chord parts that are typical of fingerstyle blues guitar.

Part Two: Rhythm Guitar Vocabulary, Patterns and Techniques

The aim of Part One of this book was to develop your finger independence in a fun and musical way. You have now mastered lots of important vocabulary and should be getting a feel for keeping a 1/4 note bass line steady while playing intricate licks and lines.

Part Two of this book looks in much greater detail at the art of fingerstyle blues rhythm guitar and the skills and techniques needed to build confidence and fluency in this demanding genre.

The work you have done on 1/4 note pedal tone bass will come in very handy here, but do be aware that you should still work through the exercises and songs in this section very slowly. There is still some way to go in developing picking hand syncopation, and some challenging ideas in the fretting hand too.

This section covers:

- *Chord progressions*
- *Root and octave thumb patterns*
- *Root and 5th thumb patterns*
- *Finger Picking Patterns*
- *Arpeggio bass lines*
- *Chord fragments and inversions*
- *Combining melody and chords*
- *Turnarounds*
- *Bass lines and chords*
- *Soloing and using fills while playing rhythm*
- *Using licks and riffs as chords*

After working through this section you will be well on your way to playing accomplished fingerstyle blues guitar rhythm and combining it with the soloing ideas from Part One.

Go slowly and make sure *you* are in control of your fingers. A question that has always stuck with me is 'Do you want to be the dog, or do you want to be the tail?' In other words, do you want to wag your tail, or do you want be wagged?

The way to make sure we are the boss is to practice slowly enough that our brain, not our fingers is in charge of every note.

Chapter Seven: Chords, Strumming and Basic Patterns

Throughout the years, fingerstyle blues guitar has been played on different types of guitars and in different tunings. The most common tunings are the 'standard' E tuning that you are probably using now on a six-string guitar, and 'Drop D' tuning, where the bass string is tuned down from an E to a D.

There is also DADGAD tuning, where the strings are tuned in this sequence of notes.

However, there are also some fairly rare and obscure tunings that have been used. For example, the early blues pioneer Leadbelly used a twelve-string guitar that was dropped in pitch either down to 'low C' or even 'low B', as did Blind Willie McTell.

Vestapol (DADF#AD) tuning, where the whole guitar is tuned to a D chord was also not uncommon amongst slide players such as Blind Willie[2] Johnson.

For simplicity and accessibility, this book is going to show you how to play fingerstyle blues rhythm in 'standard' E tuning, E A D G B E, as all the ideas in this book are transferable and many of the techniques can be used with a variety of different tunings.

In standard tuning, the two most common keys for fingerstyle blues are E and C due to them providing convenient access to many important bass line ideas.

We will begin by looking at the basic chords in an E Blues. They are shown with both Major and Dominant 7 voicings as these tend to be used interchangeably. '7' chords have a tenser, blusier quality, so practice both voicings and decide what you like the sound of. Occasionally it is important to play a dominant 7 voicing as it gives you a spare finger to add a melody phrase.

Basic Blues Chord Voicings

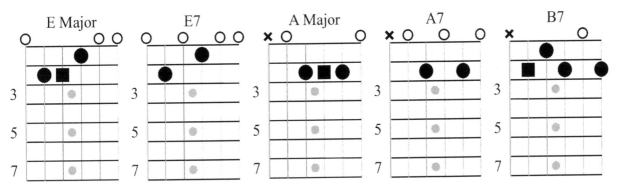

While most people associate the blues with the classic twelve-bar structure, this was actually a later innovation and is fairly uncommon in early blues. Often whole songs were formed from one- or two-note riffs over a single chord so almost any idea from Part One could be adapted for this purpose.

However, to develop your fingerpicking style it is important to learn the following patterns and chord structures around specific sequences so that you learn to coordinative both hands and change chords easily and smoothly. Be aware that any fingerpicking or strumming pattern can be applied to any sequence.

---

[2] If you want to become a truly great fingerstyle blues guitar player it is essential to change your name to Blind Willie.

We will begin, however, with the eight bar blues structure you learnt in Part One. Here it is again to refresh your memory.

'Standard' Eight Bar Blues

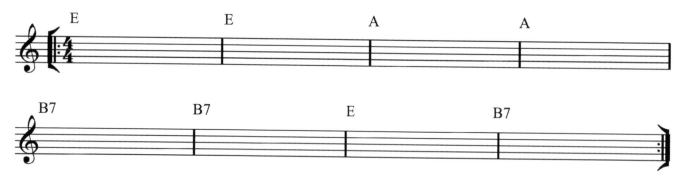

Play through this progression using one strum per bar and make sure you have memorised the sequence. Try it with both types of chord; Major and Dominant 7ths. Using a metronome set at 60bpm, gradually increase the tempo until you can confidently change chords at speed. Try playing more strums in each bar when you feel ready.

B7 may take a bit of getting used to if you've not played it before. If you're struggling, try the following, easier voicing of B7:

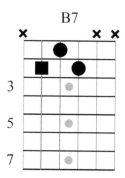

When you are feeling comfortable with these changes, introduce the first strumming pattern.

Start by following the strumming pattern arrows shown in the example, use your index fingernail to play the bass string and the pad of the index finger to play the up strum on the chord. This is sometimes called a *brush stroke*.

Next, alter your approach so that you are picking the bass note with your thumb and using three fingers together to pluck the higher part of the chord.

Where there are four notes notated in a chord, be selective about which three notes you choose to pluck. It's normally best to aim for the higher strings.

Example 7a:

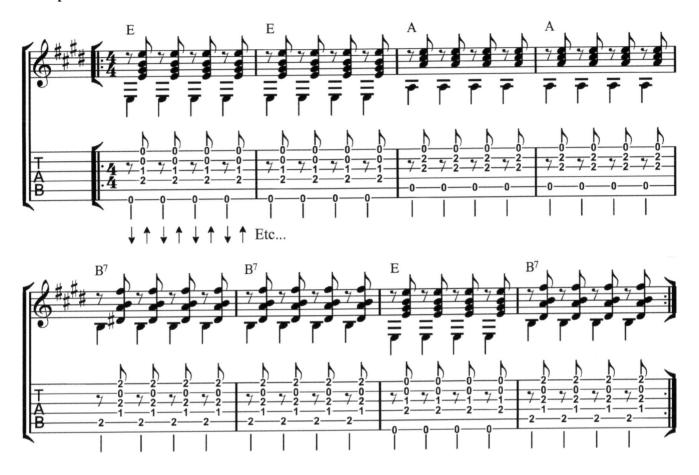

The next strumming example is an important rhythm to know and is sometimes referred to as a *freight train* rhythm, as it mirrors the sound of an engine locomotive. It's quite common in country guitar playing too. I've only written it out on the E chord below, but you should transfer this pattern to the other chords in the progression and the ones later in this chapter.

Keep the wrist soft and light and try to move the strums from the middle to the higher strings as you can hear on the track. The only thing set in stone is the pounding bass note on the beat.

Example 7b:

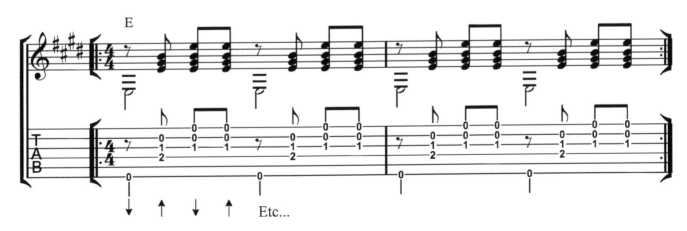

When you are fluent with this progression and can play it with both strums and thumb and fingers, it is time to move on to studying some finger picking patterns.

The most important picking pattern to master, as it underpins more than ninety percent of the fingerstyle blues approach, is the *alternating bass* picking pattern. In this style, the thumb is used to alternate between two bass notes, normally the root and its octave or the root and the 5th.

When playing an E chord, the root and octave are located on the sixth and fourth strings respectively.

Slowly work through the following example being sure to pay careful attention to the accuracy of your thumb and the rhythm of the music. Ensure your picking hand thumb plays the bass notes on the sixth and fourth strings, and three fingers together play the top part of the chord.

Remember also to use some palm muting or *damping* in the picking hand by resting the palm slightly down on the bass strings. This will keep the bass tight and crisp and help it to cut through the chords. Listen for this on the audio tracks.

Example 7c:

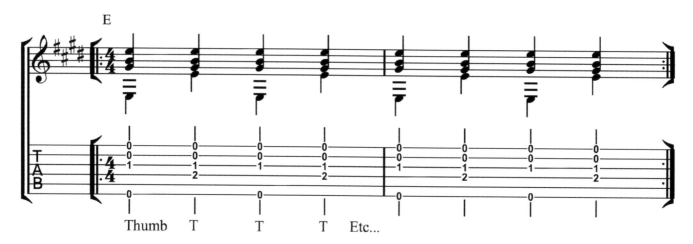

Staying with the same idea, let's move the chord to the off-beat to create a different, livelier effect.

Example 7d:

On other types of chord it is not always practical to play the root and octave. For example, on an open 'A' chord the bass often moves between the root and 5th on the fourth string. Check out the following pattern and careful of the change from A to A7 in bar two.

Example 7e:

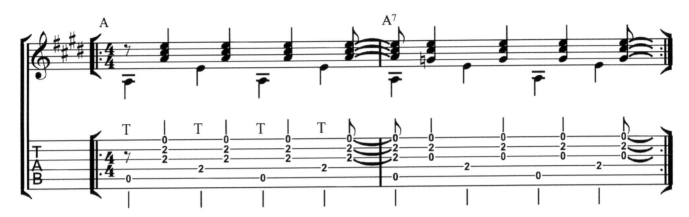

The 5th of A (E) can also be played on the sixth string *below* the root. This can get a bit 'country' though, so be careful!

Example 7f:

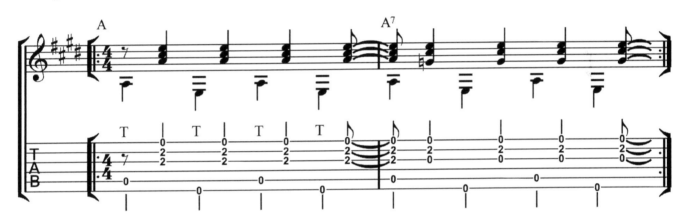

The B7 chord can also be played with a bass on the fifth and fourth strings.

Example 7g:

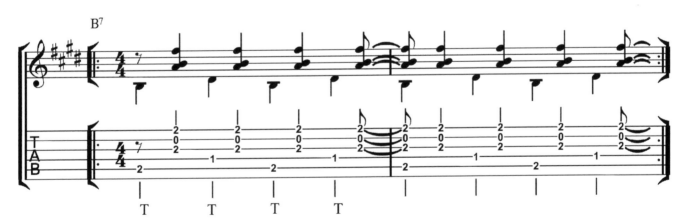

As the independence of your thumb begins to develop, try the following exercise with a simple E Major chord. You begin with the chord on the beat in the first bar and switch to playing them on the off-beat in the second bar.

Example 7h:

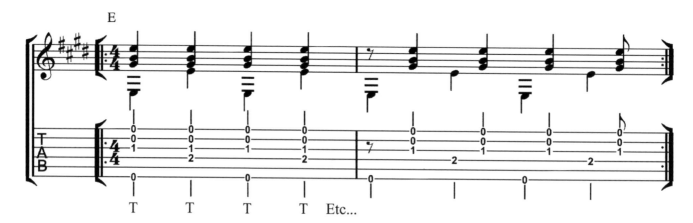

Next, try creating syncopated rhythms by combining on- and off-beat chord stabs in the same bar. This is the beginning of soloing and playing chords at the same time as it develops a huge amount of control in the picking hand.

Example 7i:

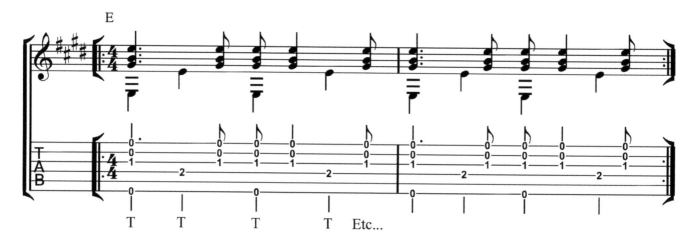

Practice the same rhythmic idea on the A and B7 chords too, before combining them together into longer progressions. The following example moves between the chords of E and A7.

Example 7i:

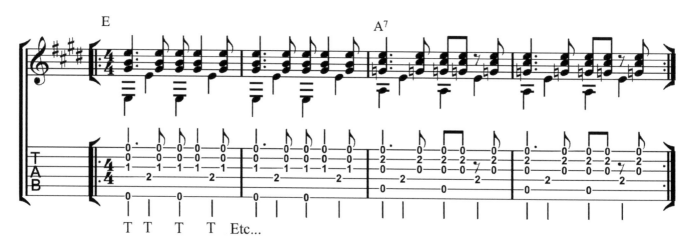

Now try a similar example that gets you used to slightly altering chords while playing a picking pattern.

Example 7j:

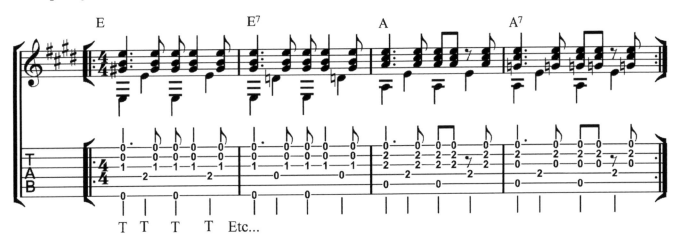

Repeat the previous nine exercises using the chords of G, C and D, and their dominant 7 equivalents. The following example will show you the most common bass note patterns to use on each chord type.

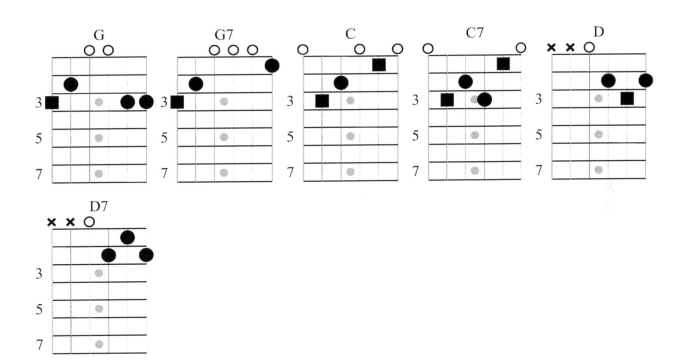

Example 7k:

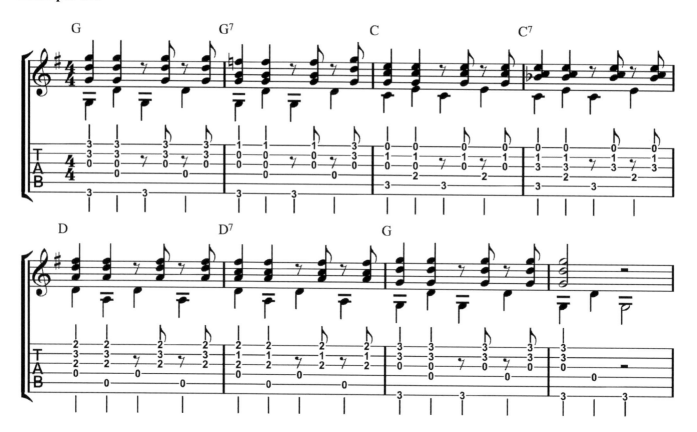

Finger Picking Patterns

The next stage in the development of the picking hand is to master some important patterns. These patterns will gradually develop into more intricate ideas and build to give you complete independence and control between your thumb and fingers.

As a general tip, should something go wrong while you're playing a picking pattern (especially live!), then the most important part of the pattern to keep going is the bass line. The listener will almost always hear a faltering bass line before they hear any inconsistency in the melody fingers.

These first exercises maintain a constant 1/4 note movement on one string with the thumb to help you focus on coordinating your picking fingers. Be sure to observe the correct fingering indicated above the music.

M = Middle

I = Index

R = Ring

Hold down an E Major chord when you play the following examples:

Example 7l:

Apply the above finger picking pattern to the chords of A, B7, G, A and D before moving on.

Now try this next example:

Example 7m:

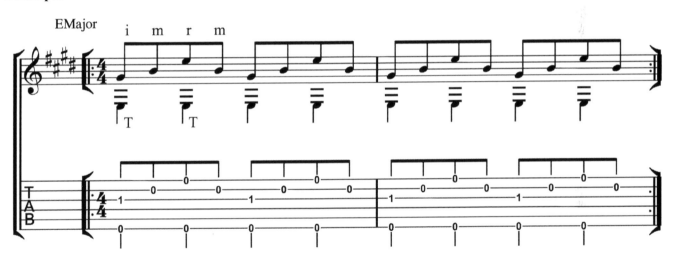

Again, move this pattern through the chords mentioned above.

The following picking idea introduces a double-stop. Use the middle and index fingers to play the two notes together.

Example 7n:

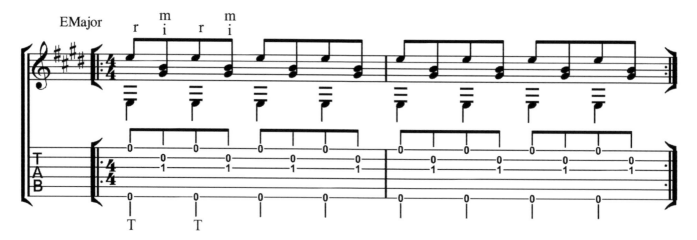

Now reverse that pattern.

Example 7o:

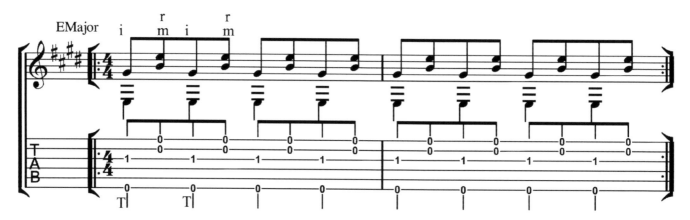

As you develop your control and fluency by gradually increasing the speed of the previous picking exercises with a metronome, it is time to reintroduce the alternating bass figure with your thumb. Remember to keep the sixth string slightly palm muted for a bluesy, percussive effect. The first two picking patterns are shown below with an added alternated bass.

The thumb is the 'engine' in this style of music. Keep it driving, rhythmic and smooth.

Example 7p:

Example 7q:

Work through the remaining picking patterns above and apply the alternating bass pattern to them. Then, apply the alternating bass note idea to the same patterns played on the chords of A, B7, G, C and D. Remember that these chords have different alternating bass patterns then the E Major chord. Refresh your memory by referring to examples 7e-7k.

The following example shows how to adapt example 7p to an A chord.

Example 7r:

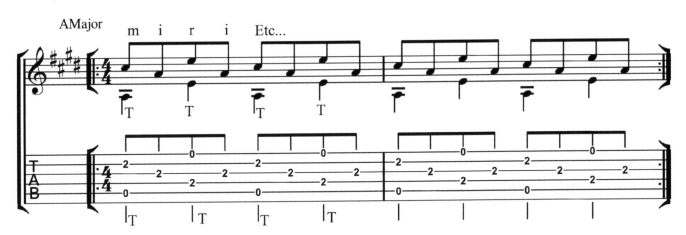

Remember, all you have to do is hold down the chord and think about the picking sequence.

Here is the same pattern adapted to the D7 chord.

Example 7s:

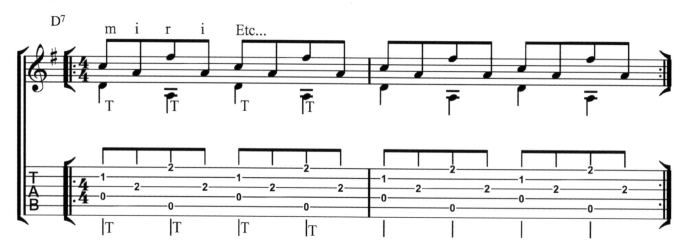

Take each pattern from examples 7l-7o and apply it to each of the chords listed above in turn. This is an important stage, as it will teach your fingers how to play the most common chords in fingerstyle blues with an alternating bass. Take your time and work methodically.

Now let's try linking up a few of these ideas into a short piece of music. Approach this study by working out the finger picking pattern on each chord first before linking each chord together.

Example 7t:

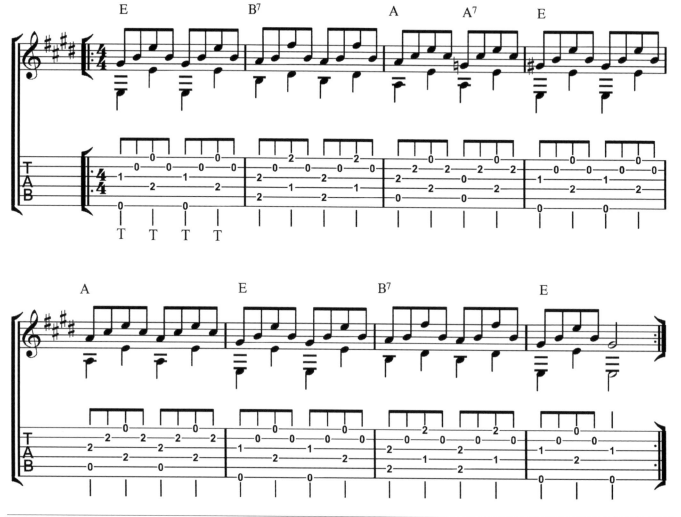

Repeat the previous etude using different picking patterns and also around the chords of G, C and D.

We have so far looked at 1/8th note picking patterns in the high part of the chord, However, something that can take a little while to become comfortable is playing 1/4 note melody notes with a 1/4 note bass line. These patterns look easy on paper, but for a lot of players they can be quite challenging at first.

Check out the following ideas.

Example 7u:

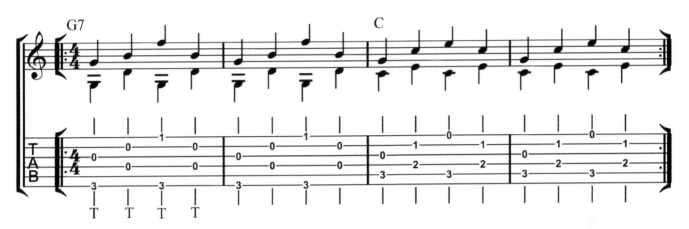

Example 7v:

Once again, apply these ideas to the other blues chords discussed in this chapter and make up some of your own patterns and chord progressions.

This chapter has provided you with a solid grounding in some important blues rhythm guitar finger picking patterns. In the next chapter, we will move on to adding melody and syncopation to these ideas to create authentic sounding, self-contained guitar parts.

Chapter Eight: Combining Melodies, Chords and Bass lines

In this chapter we will study how to combine the finger picking patterns from the previous chapter with single note melodies and solos to create a complete, stand-alone blues guitar part. The techniques in this chapter can feel quite unnatural at first, but as ever, the secret is to go slowly and be very deliberate about every note you play.

When you first try the examples in this chapter, don't worry too much about using a metronome or playing in time, just make sure that every pick is accurate. As your accuracy improves, introduce a metronome and don't forget to keep your foot stomping on the beat.

We will begin by omitting the alternating bass until you get used to adding melody notes at the top of chords. Once you master adding melody notes it is normally fairly straightforward to reintroduce the alternating bass line.

In the following example, hold down an E Major chord throughout and use your 4th finger (pinkie) to play the melody notes at the top of the chord. Ensure your thumb keeps playing the 1/4 notes on the sixth string in time.

Example 8a:

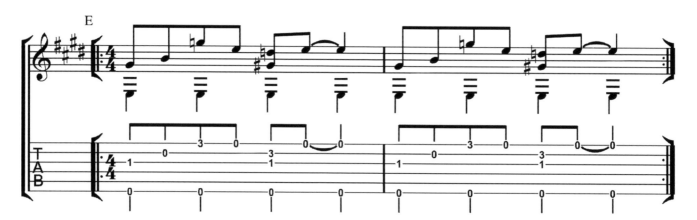

Here's a similar line played on an A chord.

Example 8b:

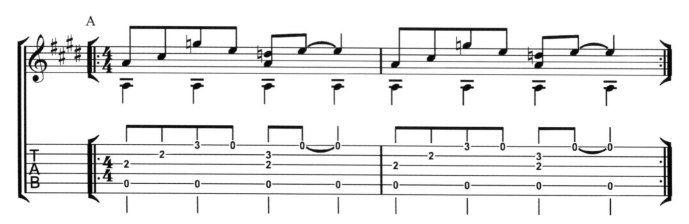

When playing in this 'open' position on the guitar, many lines that you hear on records can be found by simply experimenting with melodies using your little finger on the top two strings.

Try the next melody that begins with your 4th finger playing the 3rd fret of the second string. Hold an E Major chord throughout. Notice how I switch between single notes and double-stops to combine solo and chordal textures.

Example 8c:

Now, let's play a bend on the top G note while holding down the E Major chord. This bend might be difficult at first as you need to use your weaker 4th finger.

Example 8d:

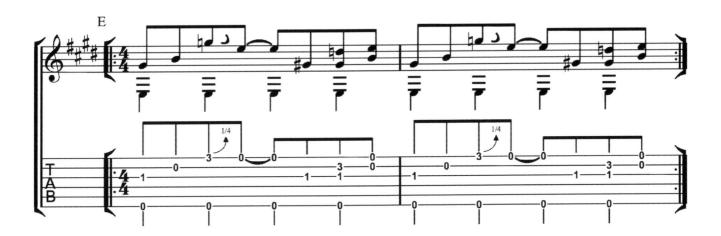

It's also worth practicing this bend on an A chord because it is easy to push the bend into the second string by accident. Use your 1st and 2nd fingers to hold down the A7 chord and use your 4th finger to play the bend on the E string and the D on beat three. Watch out for the quick change to C#.

Example 8e:

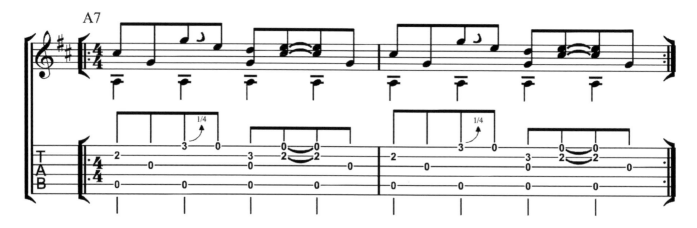

The following idea combines a hammer-on into an E chord with a bend on the top string. This is a very common movement in acoustic blues guitar.

Example 8f:

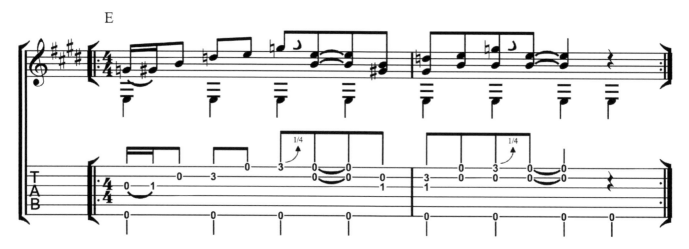

As your finger dexterity develops, you may wish to start adding faster licks to the top of chords. The following idea uses hammer-ons and pull-offs with your little finger and may take some careful practice.

Example 8g:

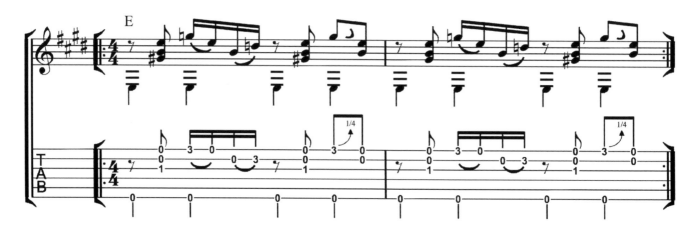

The previous examples have all started with a chord note on the beat, but it is important to experiment with playing scale notes on the beat instead. The following example shows a line around an A7 chord with the 6th (F#), as the first melody note. Use your little finger to play the notes on the top string.

Example 8h:

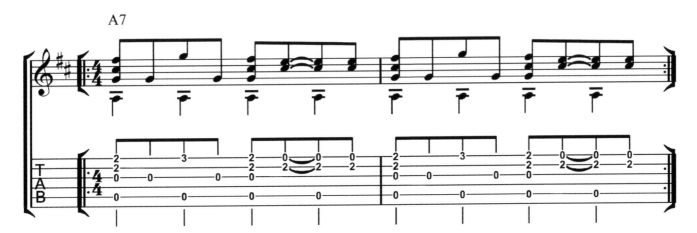

Example 8i:

Let's take a look at some common movements around the B7 chord before tying some of these ideas together into a longer etude.

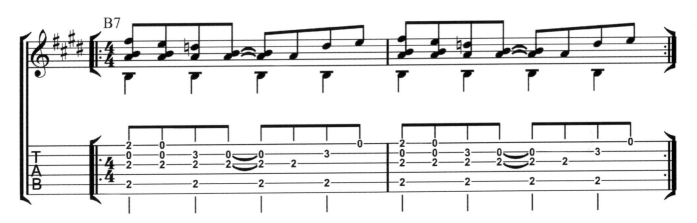

The next line may be a little tricky. Each bend is played with the little finger, and you need to be careful not to accidently touch the adjacent string with the bending finger.

Example 8j:

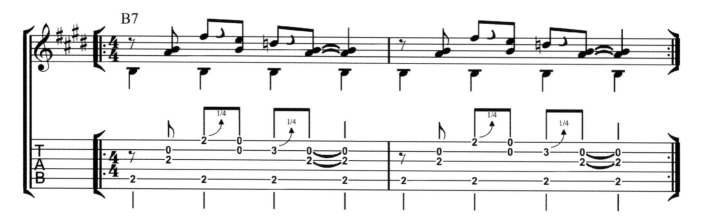

The following study will help you combine the ideas from the previous pages. Watch out for the bass line in bar six. We will look at bass lines like this in more detail later, but for now, use your 4th finger to play the low G.

Remember to hold down the chord indicated throughout each bar.

Example 8k:

Now the ideas are starting to flow, it is important that you spend time improvising and finding your own melodies to play over chords. Use the licks and vocabulary you developed in Chapters Two, Three and Four to help you.

The next stage is to begin playing these melodies and chords with the addition of the alternating bass lines we studied in Chapter Seven. This extra task requires a whole extra level of concentration at first, so as always go very slowly and make sure that you are in control of every note and thumb pick. It's extremely easy to forget about the thumb movement or mix up which string it is supposed to be hitting.

Refresh your memory of example 8c and now try it with the thumb playing an alternating bass line on the sixth and fourth strings. Hold down the E Major chord throughout, and pay attention to the thumb strokes while palm muting slightly. The goal is to make the guitar sound like two separate instruments.

Example 8l:

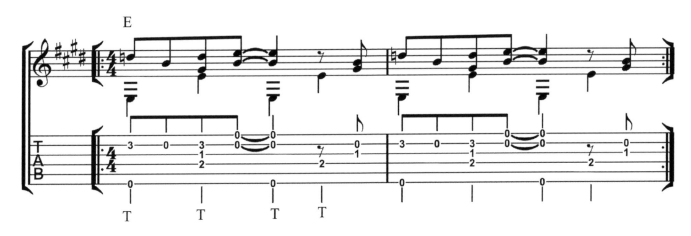

The next line starts off in a similar manner, however, there is now a fast lick on beat three. Notice how the bass note is isolated on beat four.

Example 8m:

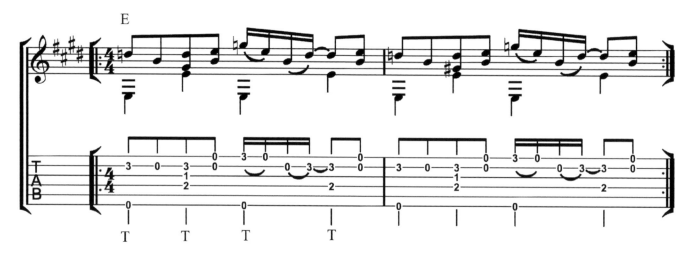

Here's an alternating bass line combined with licks on an A7 chord.

Example 8n:

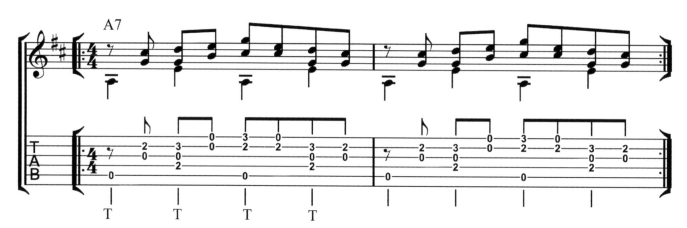

The next line should test you a little more.

Example 8o:

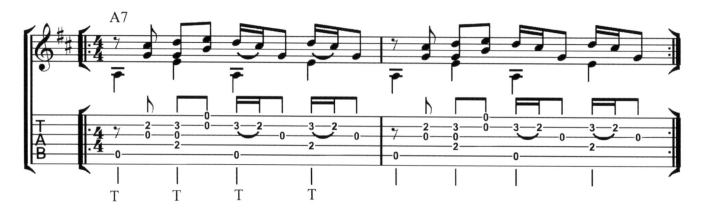

The following alternate bass lines are built on a B7 chord.

Example 8p:

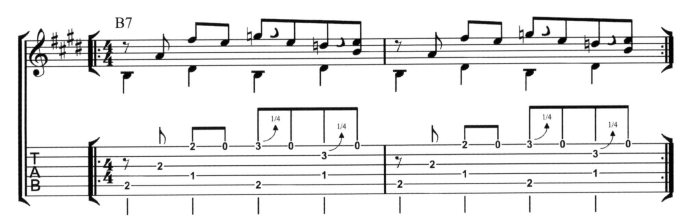

Example 8q:

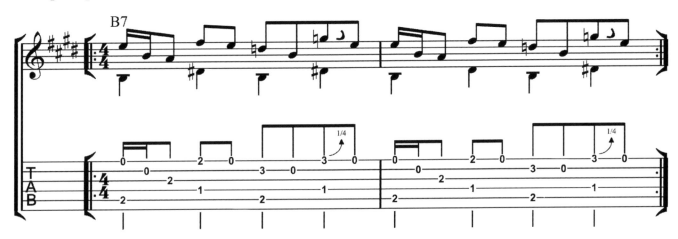

As you become more familiar with the alternating bass movement over these chords, go back to example 8k and play through it again adding in the alternating bass patterns you have worked on in the previous six examples.

Of course, there are other important chords, bass lines and vocabulary to master too, especially in the common 'blues keys' of C and A, however all of the ideas shown around the chords of E, A and B7 are easily transferrable to other keys and a lot of vocabulary will be covered in the next chapter when we look at playing movable shapes higher up the neck.

Chapter Nine: Playing up the Neck

Most of the chord work we have done so far has been played around the bottom of the guitar and used open strings. In this chapter, we will look at how to use higher voicings of chords and combine them seamlessly with the open voicings seen earlier.

As most of the following chord ideas don't use open strings, they are normally movable and can be played in different keys by shifting positions, just like scales or barre chords.

The first idea is based around an E7 chord voicing with a root on the fourth string. It can be played in the following way:

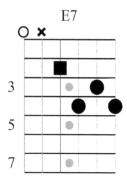

The open sixth string is still available as a low E bass note.

The following chord riff slides the notes on the top three strings down and then up a semitone while keeping the root on the fourth string constant to great a very bluesy effect. The chord voicing you are moving to looks like this:

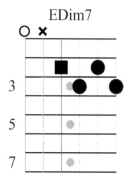

Check out the following phrase:

Example 9a:

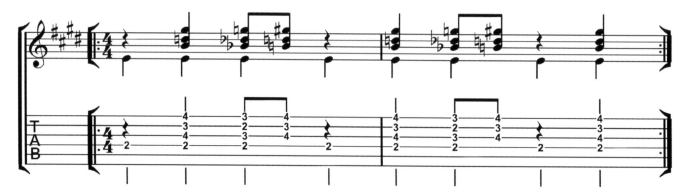

As I mentioned, the open on the sixth string root note E is still available to us so it is possible to add an alternating bass line to the previous chord movement. This line is a little awkward at first but soon becomes comfortable if you practice slowly.

Example 9b:

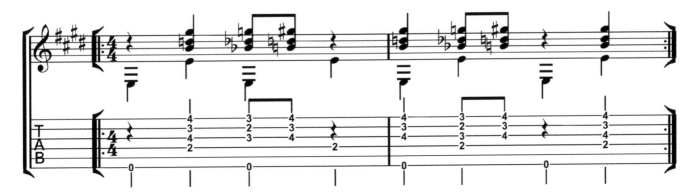

As this shape is a movable chord, we can use the open A string to play the same figure on an A7 chord.

Example 9c:

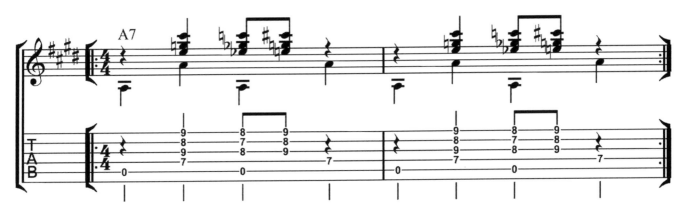

While there is normally no low B string available, it is possible to move the previous idea up a tone to play a B7 chord as long as you keep the bass line on the fourth string.

Example 9d:

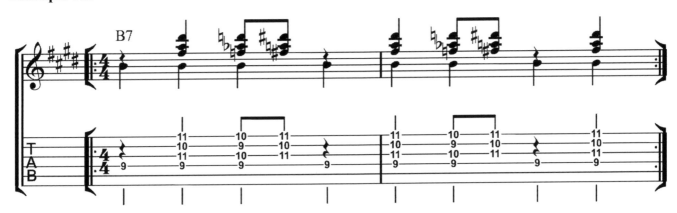

The following short figure shows how you can combine these chords into a musical idea.

Example 9e:

While I would not normally play the above sequence in its entirety, each isolated chord riff is a handy figure to mix in with other voicings of the same chord. Of course, the previous rhythms can be changed too. The next example combines an alternating bass chord and lick with the above E7 riff.

Example 9f:

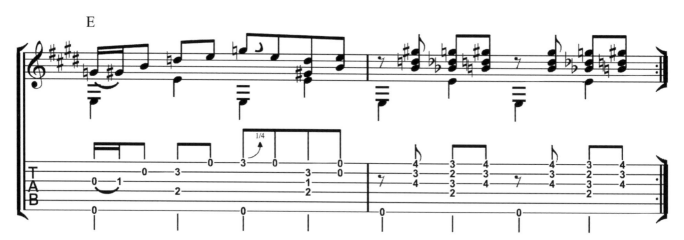

Another useful chord shape to know is based on a movable C7 shape. This chord is very common in fingerstyle blues and country as it gives access to a root and 5th alternating bass line anywhere on the neck.

The chord shape is shown below with the roots of E, A and B7.

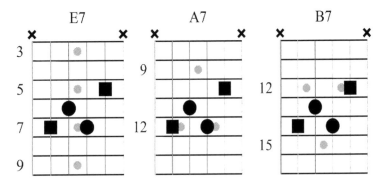

These shapes are very useful for fingerpicking patterns and it's easy to add an alternating bass on the sixth string by simply moving the 3rd finger to form the following shape:

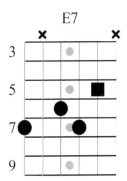

Check out this next finger picked example. While it's a bit 'country' it is a great exercise and can be easily be adapted with any of the patterns in Chapter Seven. Hold down the chords above throughout the example and only move your 3rd finger.

Example 9g:

This shape also gives us a bit of an opportunity to have some fun and create an alternate bass line on the bottom *three* strings. This example is similar in some ways to the previous idea, but your thumb plays any note on the sixth, fifth or fourth string.

Example 9h:

It can also be useful to play fragments of standard barre chords that allow us to combine chordal playing with lead work and move these ideas around the neck.

The following lines are based around the full barre chord of A Major, but it is worth beginning with the small fragment shown.

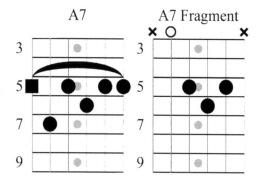

Start by playing the following few licks to give you an idea of where common melody notes lie around these shapes.

In this first lick, barre the second, third and fourth string at the fifth fret. Notice that the alternating bass movement is now between the root and b7 (G), not the root and octave.

Example 9i:

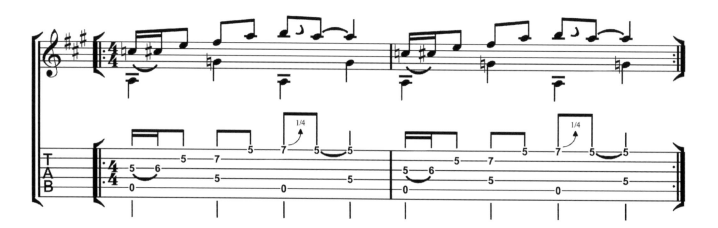

The next line combines the A7 chord fragment with an alternating bass line and a lick with a triplet feel.

Each of the chords is *raked* by rolling the fingers of the picking hand across the strings. Begin with the thumb and fingers on the strings and remove them in quick succession.

Example 9j:

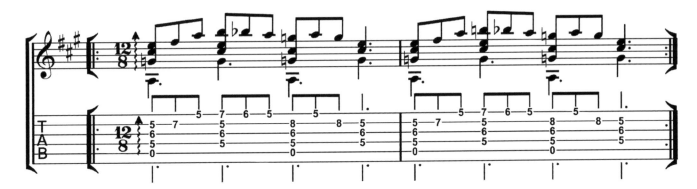

Try sliding the previous two licks up two frets to play them over the chord of B7. You'll need to barre right across the guitar with your first finger to play the low B note in the bass.

Example 9k:

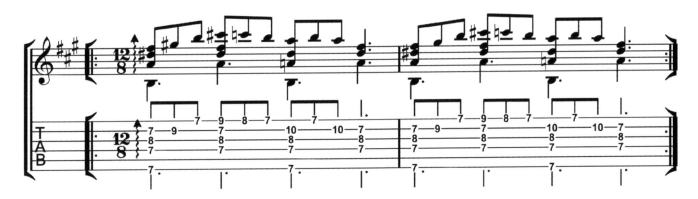

These movable chord forms are extremely useful as they allow you to play in any key, and help you to access notes that are higher up the neck whilst keeping forward momentum in the music with chords and bass lines.

Voicings and Inversions

Another way fingerstyle blues players access notes and chords higher up the neck is to use different *voicings* and *inversions* of the same chord. For example, the chord of E Major can be played in the following three ways:

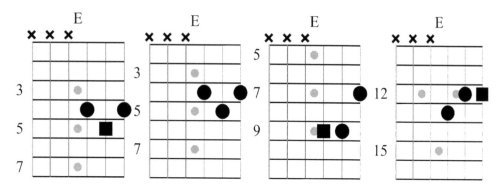

The following triplet idea links these shapes together while playing a 1/4 note bass line. I've also added some authentic semitone slides into each chord. These slides can be applied to any chord you play.

Example 9l:

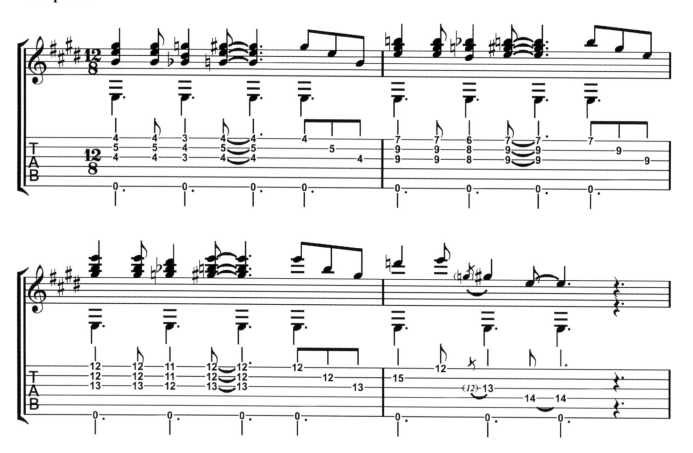

These major shapes are very useful, and you should experiment to find ways to make them your own, but to make them bluesier they can be converted to dominant 7 chords by lowering the high root note by a tone:

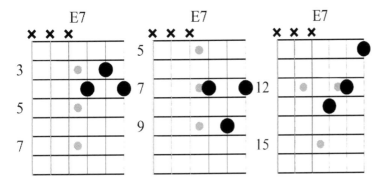

Play through the example on the previous page and use these voicing instead of the ones written.

The secret to integrating these chord fragments into your lead playing is to find single line vocabulary that you can base around each shape.

The following three examples show you a line for each chord inversion, but you can easily use any line from Part One of this book.

Example 9m:

Example 9n:

Example 9o:

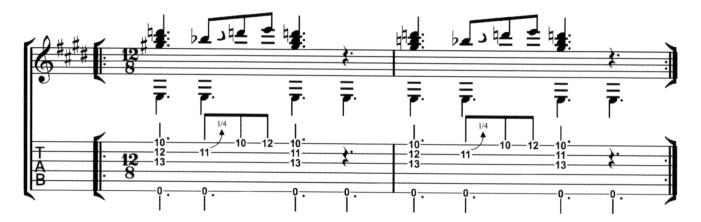

These fragments can, of course, be used to play any chord and enable us to move between closely voiced inversions of any chord in a blues sequence.

Here are the same three-note voicings for the chords of A7 and B7. I have shown the roots as hollow squares for your reference, but they are not played.

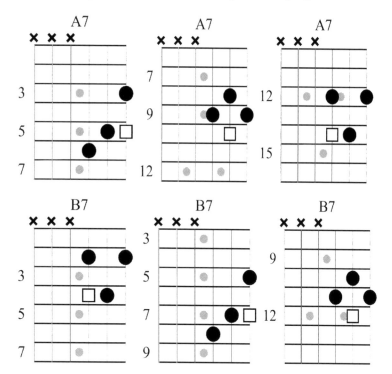

The following example shows you some ideas to link these fragments together over a blues progression around the seventh fret. Try transferring these ideas to the other positions on the neck and finding your own ways to link them.

Example 9p:

Another way to play up the neck is to use smaller two-string fragments. These notes normally come from a minor pentatonic scale. If you are playing in E, then the fragments come from E Minor Pentatonic. The following lick demonstrates the most common positions and approaches to using Minor Pentatonic fragments combined with an open E chord. **Example 9q:**

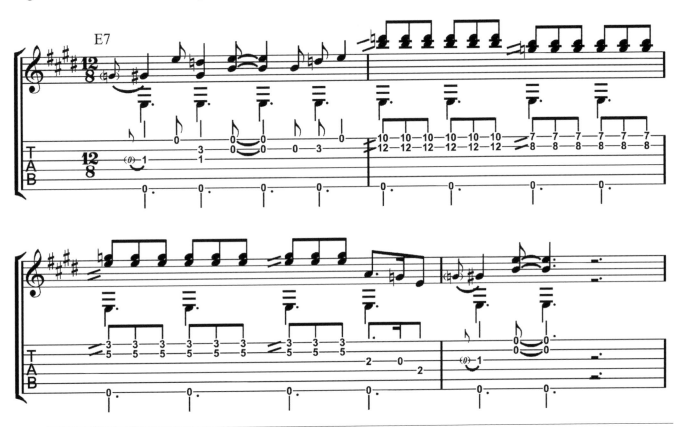

Another way to use these fragments is as short fills between open chord riffs. This is shown in the next example.

Example 9r:

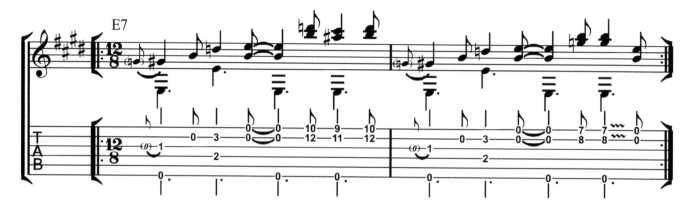

Experiment as much as possible and listen to fingerstyle blues. You'll hear ideas similar to this all the time.

One of the most distinctive features of a blues is the *turnaround* section of the tune. This occurs in the final few bars or beats of the blues form and 'turns the song around' back to the beginning. We will be looking at turnarounds and endings in the next chapter.

Chapter Ten: Turnarounds, Endings, and Bass Lines

Turnarounds normally take place over the last two bars of a blues and serve to provide a catchy *hook* at the end of the song's form. They help the listener know when the tune is about to start again (or end), and act as a waypoint between verses.

The best way to get a feel for turnarounds is simply to learn some. There are some basic common formulas to their structure and once you have memorised a few they are easy to improvise with and great fun to play.

Any turnaround can also become an *ending* by simply altering the last few beats, as you will see later. Begin by learning the following examples.

Example 10a:

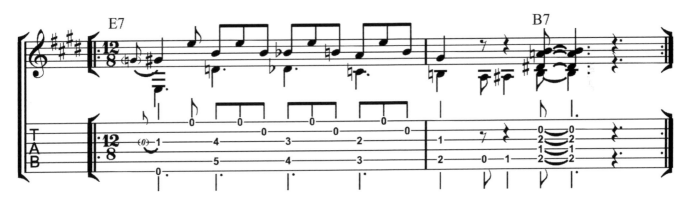

Example 10b is one of the most commonly played turnarounds. You will hear it all the time!

Example 10b:

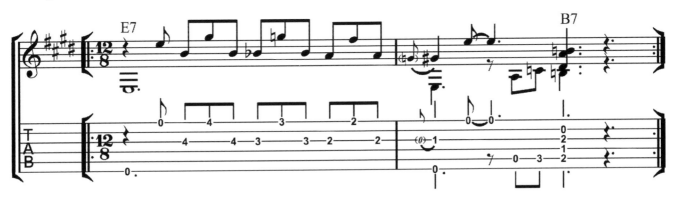

The next turnaround uses a device called contrary motion. The bass ascends, and the melody descends. This example is deceptively tricky, so take your time and learn each position change as a single unit before linking them together.

Example 10c:

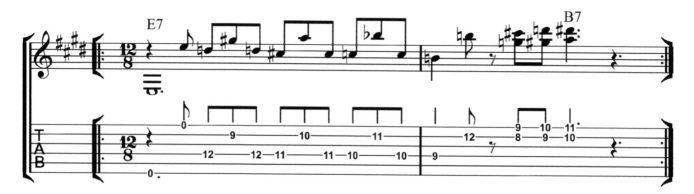

Example 10d:

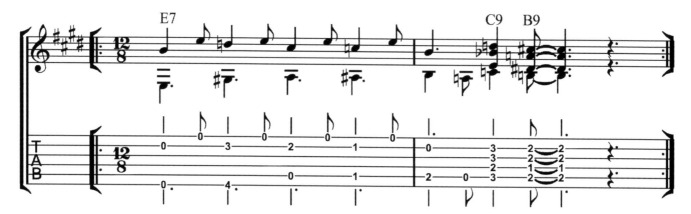

The next lick is a common line that descends under a high E pedal tone.

Example 10e:

This line involves contrary motion on the top two strings. The double-stops can either be played together or arpeggiated.

Example 10f:

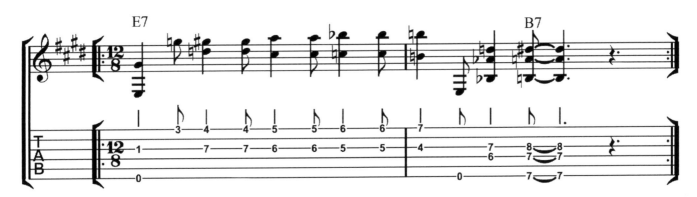

The next example is quite hard. Make sure you can comfortably finger the chord on beat two before you learn the line.

Example 10g:

As I mentioned above, any turnaround can be changed into an ending fairly easily. All you need to do is target an E chord in the final bar instead of a B7. The first idea resolves to an E7 chord from a semitone below.

Example 10h:

Can you hear how this lick now has a very 'final' quality to it? You can accentuate this by slowing down throughout the phrase until you get to the end.

The next idea converts the turnaround in example 10d to an ending by approaching an E9 chord from a semitone above (F9).

Example 10i:

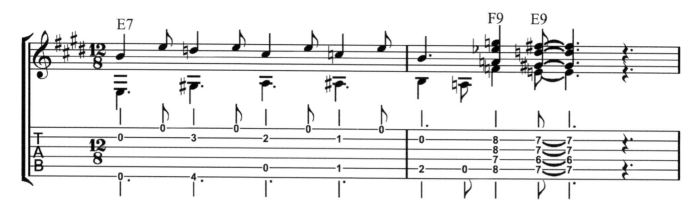

To help you learn to feel when the turnaround should be played, learn this full twelve-bar blues study in the style of Big Bill Broonzy and try out different turnarounds in the last two bars.

Example 10j:

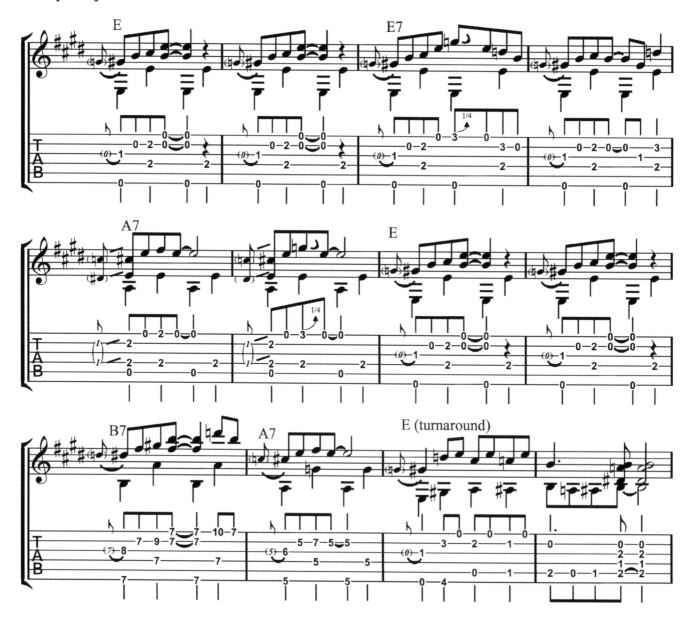

Bass Lines with Chords

A technique that you will hear in more advanced fingerstyle blues is the combination of an arpeggiated bass line with syncopated chord *stabs*. These ideas can sound a little 'Boogie Woogie' but they are played quite regularly in the blues.

Start by learning the following bass line and make sure you are extremely confident with it before moving on.

Example 10k:

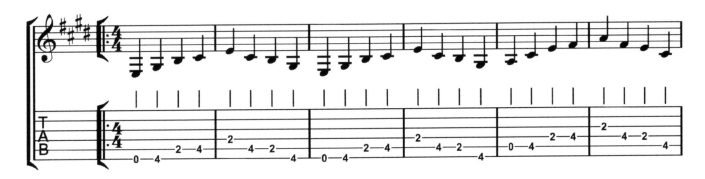

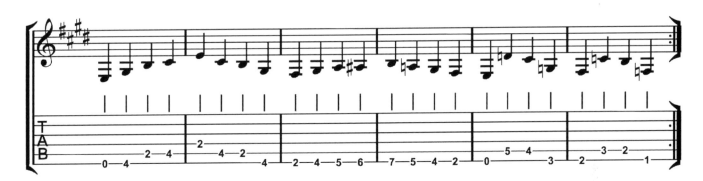

The next stage is to master the rhythm of the syncopated chord stabs. I recommend that you do this with just an open E string in the bass to begin with.

Example 10l:

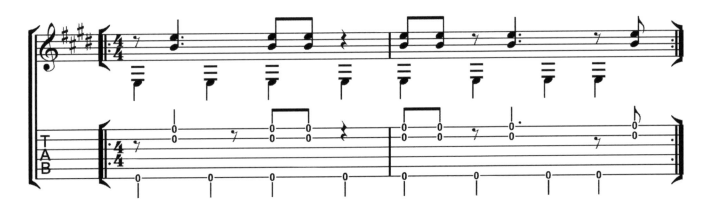

Now add in the bass line for the first two bars.

Example 10m:

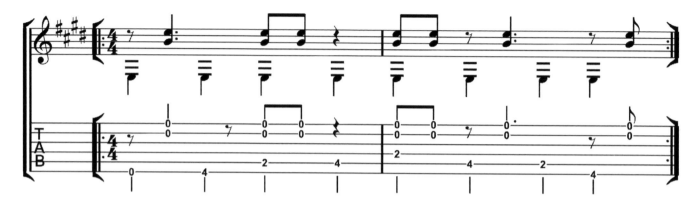

Now try to work slowly through the whole form and combine these ideas together.

Example 10n:

In the final, two-bar turnaround section, make sure you play each single bass note with the finger you will use to play the lowest note of the following chord. For example, use your 2nd finger to play the bass notes D and C# (5 and 4) in the penultimate bar.

If you want to get *really* adventurous, you can start to add in the odd lead lick while playing the bass line and stabs. This technique normally requires a lot of advanced planning due to some awkward fingerings. Start by adding just one melody note, as shown in the next example.

Example 10n:

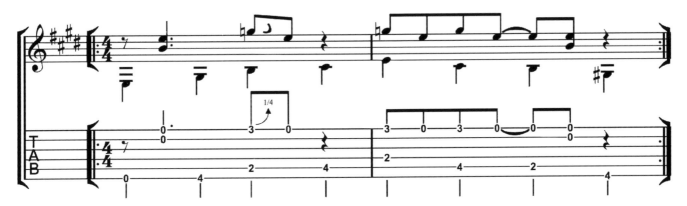

When this type of idea makes sense to your fingers, slowly try to add some more notes to the solo.

Example 10o:

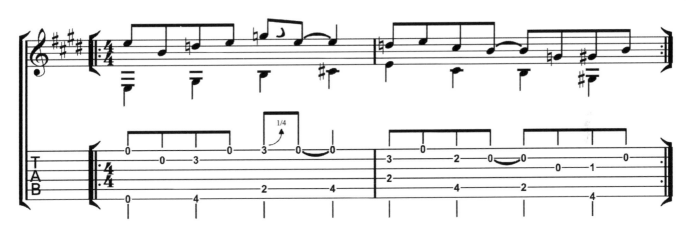

As your confidence builds, begin to add short solo phrases to each chord, making sure that the bass line is solid and in time. By now you should be getting a feel for how to create your own blues licks with the pentatonic scale, but feel free to borrow ideas from part one to get you started.

Above all, use your ears and copy ideas from your favourite fingerstyle guitarists.

Studies

This book has covered a huge amount of material, and I hope it gives you many hours of happy study. I've tried to cover as many of the rudiments, techniques and approaches as possible while focusing on vocabulary. By deconstructing the style, the goal is that you are able to recreate what you hear on records and write or improvise your own fingerstyle acoustic blues music.

The following two studies tie many of these features together and will form the basis of your own songs. Go slow and have fun!

Example 11a:

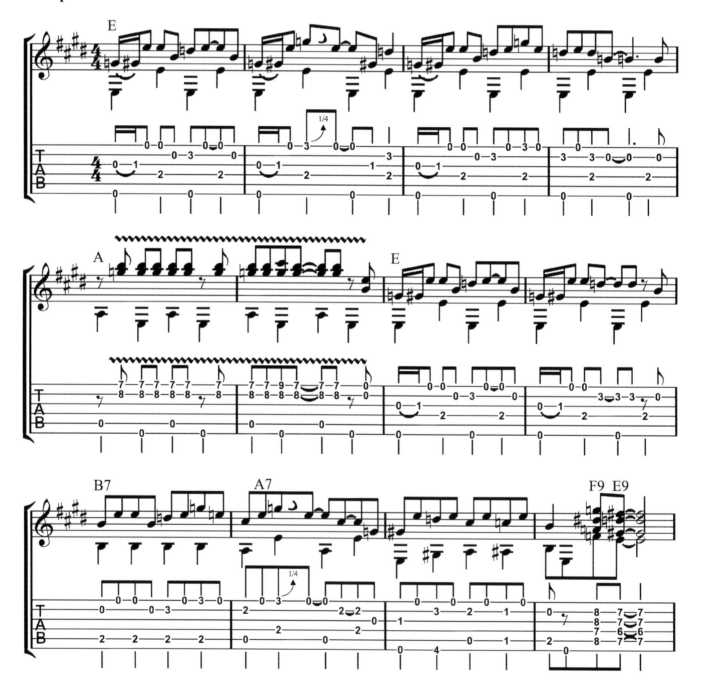

This next study is in the key of A and uses a static bass note throughout.

Example 11b:

Essential Listening

The following list of titles is far from exhaustive but represents a good cross section of music you should get your hands on. Due to the nature of the copyright on these recordings, there are many great quality 'best of' albums and there is sure to be one of your favourite musician. There are also many recordings released as 'Library of Congress Sessions' that were recorded to preserve early roots music.

Roy Book Binder - Don't Start Me Talkin'....
Mississippi John Hurt - D.C. Blues Vol.1 & 2
Rev. Gary Davis – The Guitar and Banjo of...
John Mooney - Dealing With the Devil
John Hammond - Live
Blind Boy Fuller - East Coast Piedmont Style
Pink Anderson - Vol. 2 Medicine Show Man
Big Bill Broonzy - Warm, Witty & Wise
Son House - The Real Delta Blues
Charley Patton - The Essential Collection
Blind Lemon Jefferson - The Complete Recordings / Best Of
Robert Johnson - The Complete Recordings
Blind Willie McTell - The Early Years / The Legendary Library of Congress Recordings
Blind Blake - All the Published Sides
Mississippi Fred McDowell - My Home is in the Delta
Elisabeth Cotton - Live!
Blind Willie Johnson - The Essential Blind Willie Johnson
Lightnin Hopkins - Double Blues

There are literally hundreds of early blues albums that have been compiled or remastered. YouTube is also a great source of inspiration as many people have put together long playlists you can listen to. If a musical idea jumps out at you, then steal it and make it your own. Then you too can become part of the long genealogy of the blues.

Enjoy the journey.

Joseph

Made in the USA
Columbia, SC
03 September 2020